Time-limited Psychody
Psychotherapy with Ch
and Adolescents

CW00959577

At a time when there is increasing concern about the escalation of child and adolescent mental health problems, *Time-limited Psychodynamic Psychotherapy with Children and Adolescents* provides an innovative contextual model that engages the child or young person and their parents. The core of the model is the recognition of the dynamic capacity for growth in the child and how this, in itself, creates opportunities for effective treatment over a relatively short period of time.

Based on evidence that the most enduring therapeutic outcomes involve a shift in the parents' relational understanding of themselves, as well as a change in the child, the book uses case examples to show how this model can be applied in everyday therapeutic practice.

Time-limited Psychodynamic Psychotherapy with Children and Adolescents is aimed at practitioners in the field of child, adolescent, parent and family psychotherapy. It will interest psychologists, child psychotherapists, doctors, psychiatrists, social workers and mental health workers.

Ruth Schmidt Neven, PhD is a child psychotherapist, clinical psychologist, educator and researcher. She trained at the Tavistock Clinic in London and over four decades has brought a pioneering approach to clinical work with children and young people, emphasising the essential nature of the meaning of behaviour.

Time-limited Psychodynamic Psychotherapy with Children and Adolescents

An interactive approach

Ruth Schmidt Neven

Routledge
Taylor & Francis Group

LONDON AND NEW YORK

First published 2017
by Routledge
2 Park Square, Milton Park, Abingdon, Oxon OX14 4RN

and by Routledge
711 Third Avenue, New York, NY 10017

Routledge is an imprint of the Taylor & Francis Group, an informa business

© 2017 Ruth Schmidt Neven

The right of Ruth Schmidt Neven to be identified as author of this
work has been asserted by her in accordance with sections 77 and
78 of the Copyright, Designs and Patents Act 1988.

All rights reserved. No part of this book may be reprinted or
reproduced or utilised in any form or by any electronic, mechanical,
or other means, now known or hereafter invented, including
photocopying and recording, or in any information storage or
retrieval system, without permission in writing from the publishers.

Trademark notice: Product or corporate names may be trademarks
or registered trademarks, and are used only for identification and
explanation without intent to infringe.

British Library Cataloguing in Publication Data
A catalogue record for this book is available from the British Library

Library of Congress Cataloging in Publication Data
Names: Schmidt-Neven, Ruth, author.
Title: Time-limited psychodynamic psychotherapy with children
and adolescents : an interactive approach / Ruth Schmidt-Neven.
Description: Milton Park, Abingdon, Oxon ; New York, NY :
Routledge, 2016. | Includes bibliographical references and index.
Identifiers: LCCN 2016001727 | ISBN 9781138960930 (hbk) |
ISBN 9781138960947 (pbk) | ISBN 9781315620404 (ebk)
Subjects: LCSH: Child psychotherapy. | Brief psychotherapy for
teenagers. | Psychodynamic psychotherapy for children. |
Psychodynamic psychotherapy for teenagers.
Classification: LCC RJ504.3 .S36 2016 | DDC 618.92/8914--dc23
LC record available at http://lccn.loc.gov/2016001727

ISBN: 978-1-138-96093-0 (hbk)
ISBN: 978-1-138-96094-7 (pbk)
ISBN: 978-1-315-62040-4 (ebk)

Typeset in Sabon
by Saxon Graphics Ltd, Derby

My thanks and gratitude to the many children, parents and young people I have worked with, from whom I have learned so much.

Contents

A contextual analysis of time-limited psychodynamic psychotherapy with children, young people and parents

Introduction and overview

Psychodynamic therapy and the changing emotional and social landscape of childhood and parenthood

The 21st century presents us with challenges with respect to the way in which we disseminate information, particularly in the area of mental health. A post-modern perspective asserts that we cannot isolate a particular treatment such as time-limited psychodynamic psychotherapy for children, young people and their parents, from a broader critical reflection and examination of professional practices concerned with child and family mental health. Our perspective of our practice can also not be separated from a values and ethically based position with which it must essentially be intertwined. In work with children and young people therefore, psychotherapy and advocacy become one.

This book builds on my earlier publications and research that take a critical view of the contemporary bio-medical approach to the construction of child and adolescent mental health, often to the exclusion of the relational, family and social context. The predominance of the bio-behavioural paradigm and the loss of a developmental understanding of children's behaviour, constitute potential risk factors for children and young people, together with the increasingly reductionist approach to knowledge about childhood and parenting.

Given these challenges, what role can psychoanalysis or psychodynamic thinking play? Psychoanalysis has had to weather ongoing criticism for many years because of the apparent lack of a credible scientific evidence base for its practice. Cuts in public services have tended to push psychoanalytic treatments to the sidelines given that they have been viewed as synonymous with long-term treatment. The response from the psychoanalytic community not unreasonably, has been to attempt to justify its relevance and to expand its research and evidence base. In its eagerness to do so however, there is a risk that the very methodologies used such as outcome studies, manualisation of treatments, and the reaching after the holy grail of the randomised controlled trial, actually reinforce the de-contextualised problems for children and young people described above. These methodologies will not take us to the Promised Land as they are already out of date, encased as they are within the individual pathology focused discourse that is resonant with modernity biased practices.

In this book it is not suggested that we should not conduct research or examine our professional practice, but rather that we need to take a very different view of what constitutes health and wellbeing and positive outcomes for children and young people. This book on time-limited psychodynamic psychotherapy therefore takes as its starting point the recognition that we cannot change therapeutic practice without changing or recalibrating the way in which we construct the conceptual psychodynamic framework. The term psychodynamic is used throughout the book rather than psychoanalytic, which I believe is incorrectly used as a generic descriptor when it more appropriately refers to a specific treatment mode. The recalibration of the psychodynamic framework requires more than a tweaking of established psychotherapeutic practice with children and young people in order to accommodate a shorter time frame. The oft quoted statement that it is only through the practice of long-term psychotherapy that we can successfully carry out shorter-term work is also refuted. Instead, we are concerned with reconfiguring the way in which psychodynamic ideas can be applied in a new and different way to encompass the changing emotional and social landscapes of childhood, parenting and family life. This means that we must take a fresh stance with respect to the many articles of faith that surround traditional psychotherapeutic practice and that confine many training institutions to repeating theoretical doctrines when these may no longer be applicable. We need to open the windows and allow space for the development of fresh theory and practice to emerge that will be resonant with the needs of today's child and today's family.

The focus in time-limited psychodynamic psychotherapy with children, parents and young people thus requires a total review of who is there to be worked with/what is the primary task and how can one best go about it? These questions are all underpinned by the meaning of the symptom or behaviour that is presented. A core theme of the book is that by acknowledging that in the first instance, the therapeutic task is to uncover meaning rather than pathology, we begin to recognise the enormous value of the symptom. In other words the symptom is *the opportunity* that opens up a wider, richer way of working. Because of this, therapeutic work with parents, caregivers and the wider network has equal value to that of work solely with the child and young person.

By *widening the therapeutic frame* in therapeutic work with children, young people and their parents in this way, we reflect the world that they actually inhabit. This approach is the antithesis of a traditional therapeutic approach that is entirely focused on therapy with the child and young person, in which the role of parents and others is perceived as marginal and as primarily that of 'supporting' the child or young person's therapy. One may argue that these rigidities and inward looking practices have, even more than the apparent lack of research rigour, served to undermine support for a psychodynamic way of working, particularly in the public services.

The integrated approach suggested in this book requires a high level of skill and experience as practitioners need to be equally adept at working with parents as well as with children and young people. This requires a change in the way in which training is offered and how students are selected. The approach described in this book is the opposite of single strand thinking and is reliant on a confluence of experiences and ideas. One of the often observed side-effects of traditional psychoanalytic and psychotherapeutic training is that the life of the student that has gone before is considered a mere stepping stone on the road to psychoanalytical enlightenment. One may have observed fellow students with previously rich and demanding careers that appear to have become negated with the taking on of the identity of psychotherapist or psychoanalyst. In recalibrating the psychodynamic approach we would want instead to integrate, encourage and use the previous experience of the practitioner as a powerful source of information, depth and diversity.

With respect to my own experience, the gestation for this book has in a sense taken all of my professional life and it may be said to represent a distillation of the experience I have had of working with children, parents, families and young people in a wide variety of settings and across three continents, the United Kingdom, South Africa and Australia. It has been clear to me in the course of writing this book how influential these different opportunities for learning have been and how they come together to inform my current practice. I commenced my career as a graduate of psychology, but continued to work for several years as a social worker initially in the field of child protection and subsequently as a psychiatric social worker in adult psychiatry and then in child and adolescent mental health services. My own personal analysis and training as a child psychotherapist opened up a world of knowledge and understanding. Finally, I have come full circle back to the field of psychology in which I carried out my PhD research. A substantial part of this professional experience put me in touch with children, young people and adults struggling with high levels of stress, abuse and chaos in their lives. This presented an enormous challenge in terms of being able to find ways of making even the slightest difference in the face of major intergenerational deprivation and trauma. It brought home to me that the individually lived life cannot be separated from the relational, family, systemic and wider organisational, social and political environment. It further brought home to me that the predominantly pathology-driven diagnoses associated with these problems have not led to the hoped-for outcomes with respect to improvements in child and family mental health. In fact it may be argued that narrow pathology-based diagnoses not only compromise the child and young person, but also the ability of professionals to offer meaningful treatment and support.

It is here of course, that psychodynamic understanding comes into its own. The paradox is that at a time when psychodynamic practices and services are coming under threat we need this wealth of understanding more than ever. Psychodynamic understanding predicated as it is on the meaning of behaviour, on observation and on lines of continuity, presents us with a highly contemporary and engaging method. This method as described in the book demonstrates the intersection between the intra-psychic, the inter-personal and the systemic, where none of these fields can be kept artificially separate from one another in the therapeutic encounter. It enables us to shift from a pre-ordained prescriptive diagnostic framework to one in which we validate and promote the inherent knowledge of the people we are trying to help. For children and young people in particular, the recognition of their inherent capacity for health and growth is intrinsic to the process. Professionals in turn are able to move from the servicing of deficit-focused stratagems that preclude critical judgement, to drawing on their deeper well of understanding, insight and skill.

Finally, where does this lead us in the future? Time-limited psychodynamic psychotherapy presents us with a different view not only of time, but also of what we mean by 'illness' and by 'cure'. Time-limited psychodynamic psychotherapy is not in any way presented here as a cost-cutting measure. However, once we move away from a predominantly bio-medical framework, this opens up opportunities for a different way of engaging with research. How the research is carried out will also need to be recalibrated in a way that can include children, young people and their parents as active participants in the inquiry. For example, involving children, young people and their parents directly in research as contributors to the process, rather than as carriers of symptomatology, has the potential not only to deliver reliable information, but also to help shift the research paradigm into that of the important area of prevention.

A further major theme of the book is that practitioners in child and adolescent mental health have a special duty of care towards children and young people, and advocacy is intrinsic to the entire psychotherapeutic enterprise. Children and young people in need cannot wait, and it therefore behoves us as psychotherapists to be very clear about our professional and values-based position with respect to how we carry out research and who will ultimately benefit from it. It is hoped that by recognising the potential for time-limited psychodynamic psychotherapy with children, parents and young people, we shift the locus of control away from pathological constructions of individual behaviour to that of a more dynamic and contextual interchange. Hearing the voice of the child and young person with respect to their everyday lived experience within the family, school and important relationships is a critical part of this dynamic inquiry. It not only makes excellent use of the skills of child psychotherapists and other practitioners, but also enables us to use this information to provide the kinds of services for children, young people and their parents that will create a true engagement in the service of positive change.

The book is divided into two parts:

Part 1 addresses current concerns about child and adolescent mental health and the particular dilemmas presented by traditional psychoanalytical practice with children and young people. It goes on to provide an overview of the pioneering work of practitioners in time-limited psychodynamic psychotherapy with adults. This is followed by a critical assessment of contemporary developments with respect to research and outcome studies in time-limited psychodynamic psychotherapy with children and young people, with a particular focus on current research dilemmas within the post-modern age.

Part 2 presents a conceptual framework for practising time-limited psychodynamic psychotherapy with children, young people and their parents, which takes as its starting pointing the recalibration of the psychodynamic approach for current times. This is predicated on the need to attend simultaneously to the four interconnected domains of the intra-psychic, the inter-personal, the systemic and the environmental. An integrated perspective is proposed of the important findings concerning the primacy of the developmental task; understanding of attachment; the contribution of family therapy and the making of meaning and the unity of brain and mind. This framework is further underpinned by the recognition of the capacity for health and growth in children and young people. This is followed by a description of the clinical method and clinical technique in time-limited psychodynamic psychotherapy with children and young people, in which attention is paid to setting up the therapeutic frame in a way that encompasses *the total field* that surrounds the child and young person. The involvement of parents and caregivers is perceived as integral to this process. In the final chapter the implications are discussed for training, and for ways in which time-limited psychodynamic psychotherapy can contribute to changing the research paradigm from one of pathology, to that of prevention.

Chapter 1

Current concerns about child and adolescent mental health

Challenging articles of faith

Acting as advocates for the child

As practitioners we are aware of the urgent mental health needs of many of the children and young people who come to our attention. This means that we must assert the primacy of the needs of the child and young person and act as their advocates. This urgency requires first and foremost a more open and critical dialogue about how our psychotherapeutic practice can address these urgent needs. It follows that the development of new theory must emerge directly from clinical practice, experience and observation, rather than from imposing theory that adheres primarily to established orthodoxies. In this book an attempt is made to provide a fresh perspective of the rich field of psychodynamic understanding and how it can be applied to time-limited psychotherapy, not only with children and young people, but also with their parents and caregivers.

The new century has inevitably prompted a reassessment and re-evaluation of many of the accepted and traditional frameworks with respect to our understanding of the social, health, economic, political and environmental issues with which we are concerned. Psychoanalysis has not escaped this scrutiny. On the one hand, we may contend that the death of psychoanalysis is greatly exaggerated since so many psychoanalytic concepts are now integral to the web and waft of daily life as to be almost imperceptible as to their origins. On the other hand, psychoanalysis and its offshoot psychotherapy as a treatment mode have not fared so well, although the theoretical study of psychoanalysis continues to evoke interest within the academic realm. The fact that psychoanalytic or psychodynamic treatments are not generally in current favour is due at least in part to a cost-cutting economic climate. This has tended to elevate cognitive behavioural therapies as the apparently only evidenced-based cure-all, particularly as it has the advantage of being time-limited. However, there are a number of other reasons for the apparent marginalising of psychodynamic psychotherapy; the most predominant of which is the reluctance of its practitioners to fully engage with the changing social and emotional landscape in which they practise. This is a particularly critical factor for those psychotherapists who work with children, parents and families, where the issues of social change are at the tipping point, since it is within the family context and the rearing of the next generation that the demands and challenges for change are largely generated.

Why we should be concerned about instrumental treatments for children and young people: Challenging the existing paradigm

The cyclical trends that influence the way in which child and adolescent mental health problems are constructed and described are as much connected with the social and environmental context as they are with the particular child. In current times we are bombarded with high statistics citing the prevalence of a range of mental disorders in the child and adolescent population. This coincides with the paradox that at no previous time have children undergone so many assessments and tests, and been given so many diagnoses with such disappointing outcomes.

Prolific researcher Professor Sir Michael Rutter makes the point that improvements in child and adolescent psychological mental health have not kept pace with the improvements in physical health. He poses the question 'Why has this been so?' and suggests, 'If we had a proper understanding of why society has been so spectacularly successful in making things psychologically worse for children and young people, we might have a better idea as to how we can make things better in the future' (Rutter, 2002, p.15).

It may also be argued that the lack of progress in child and adolescent mental health needs to be understood within the broader context of how professionals construct child and adolescent problems, and how in turn these problems are treated. It is noteworthy that whilst we have unprecedented access to clinical knowledge and evidence from research concerning child development and the role of attachment, as well as understanding of the developing brain and its impact on personality functioning, very little of this knowledge and information appears to have found its way into the mainstream and services set up to deal with child and family mental health problems. As Stanley, Richardson and Prior (2005) point out, despite knowing more about child and youth development than we ever have known in the past, this knowledge has not been translated into providing preventative strategies and services for children and families.

The main reason for this is that for the last quarter of a century if not earlier, we have witnessed a narrowing of the theoretical, clinical and research frameworks within which child and family mental health problems are constructed. Clinical evidence and findings from research (Maton *et al.*, 2006; Prilleltensky, 2005; Schmidt Neven, 2008; Timimi, 2002) indicate a predominantly bio-medically biased approach to the construction of child and family mental health, characterised by a focus on the identification of the problem within the child, often to the exclusion of the relational, family and social context. The power of the drug industry has also played a critical role in its targeting of psychopathology 'within' the child, leading for example, to an explosion of diagnoses relating to attentional and behavioural disorders such as ADD (Attention Deficit Disorder), ADHD (Attention Deficit Hyperactivity Disorder) and ODD (Oppositional Defiance Disorder). Given careful epidemiological examination these conditions would be unlikely to be prevalent in any more than 3 per cent of the population at any given time (Schmidt Neven *et al.*, 2002). Nevertheless, they are given legitimacy by many of the professionals at the forefront of assessing and recommending treatment for children and young people.

Thus, the lack of progress in child and family mental health appears to go hand in hand with increased rates of bio-medical and pathology-based diagnoses, as well as a decontextualised and fragmented view of children's problems. This narrowing of a conceptual framework for child, adolescent and family mental health has an inevitable impact on actual clinical practice. For example, it may be represented as the difference between the utilitarian view of perceiving the child's behaviour as a noise in the system, as opposed to viewing the behaviour as having a specific meaning that can throw light on their interactive and emotional experience within the family and the wider social community. Overall, the narrowing of a conceptual clinical framework leads not only to a depleted perspective, but also to a depleted narrative both with respect to the status of childhood as well as that of parenthood.

The narrowing of the conceptual framework, within which we consider child and adolescent problems, has been accompanied by the inexorable rise of cognitive behavioural therapies for a large number of mental health problems. In particular, cognitive behavioural therapies are supported because of their claim to be the only apparently evidence-based treatment offering short-term therapeutic work. Whilst cognitive behavioural therapies may be a valid treatment option for a number of adult problems, their ever increasing usage in both the assessment and treatment of children and young people particularly as a short-term therapy, requires greater scrutiny.

The main reason for this is that cognitive behavioural therapies are intrinsically concerned with limiting the field of inquiry. With respect to the child and young person, this would generally entail attempts to eliminate the symptom or presenting problem particularly if it takes the form of challenging or difficult behaviour. This of course entirely denies the fact that the presenting problem or symptom is the means through which the child and young person 'speaks' the family and is an immeasurably rich and always accurate source of data. At a time when we are confronted with the apparently endless revelations of child sexual abuse that have gone hidden for decades, it is sobering to consider that these children and young people who were at the mercy of the abuse, were not considered to be reliable witnesses to their own experience. Moreover, in many cases their behaviour in response to the abuse was dismissed as annoying or challenging, when it is possible that it would have been the only means of communicating that was available to them, in the hope of drawing attention to their predicament.

Dissenting voices

On a more positive note there are an increasing number of dissenting voices emerging in the professional community that challenge the reductionist and fragmented view of mental health issues for adults as well as for children and young people. For example, one dissenting voice has been that of clinical psychologist Richard Bentall (2009, 2012) who argues that psychiatric treatment favouring psychotropic drugs has done little to improve the health and welfare of patients, and that continued exposure to such drugs poses a distinct danger. Bentall advocates that we need instead to pay greater attention to the impact of interpersonal relationships, in particular where these have adverse outcomes for children and young people. His 2012 meta-analysis of the research literature on childhood trauma and psychosis, points to the long-term trajectory of adverse circumstances in childhood and adolescence, and the risk this poses for later mental breakdown.

Additionally, the Division of Clinical Psychology of the British Psychological Society (2013) launched a challenge to the authors of the latest Diagnostic and Statistical Manual of Mental Disorders (DSM V) and the International Classification of Mental and Behavioural Disorders (ICD 10), which they claimed had conceptual and empirical limitations. In their position statement, the Division of Clinical Psychology argued for a paradigm shift in the way in which issues of mental health are understood. The position statement, whilst not denying the role of biology, is critical of the medicalisation–disease model of distress and behaviour. They argue further for the acknowledgment of the evidence base for psycho-social causation and multi-factorial elements to be taken into account in the process of formulation. These in particular refer to the social, cultural, personal and familial historical contexts that surround the patient and the presenting problem. The views expressed within the Division of Clinical Psychology resonate with the earlier concerns of Luyten and Blatt (2007) who questioned whether it was time to change the DSM approach to psychiatric disorders and to explore how environmental factors may be implicated in the origins of psychopathology.

The need for a refreshed vision for psychodynamic work

Given the limitations of purely behavioural and symptom-based approaches in work with children and young people, it is timely to reconsider what a psychodynamic approach has to offer. The questions that need to be asked, however, refer to the ways in which the psychodynamic approach can be redefined and recalibrated for our changing times. This would necessarily include how a psychodynamic perspective of time-limited psychotherapy can resonate with the challenges of the contemporary emotional and social landscape of childhood, adolescence and parenting.

In this book, the term psychodynamic is used rather than psychoanalytic, which is considered to be limiting in the sense that it endorses mainly long-term treatment and has the potential to give rise to confusion and misunderstanding. The term psychodynamic is perceived as incorporating psychoanalytic ideas and theory as well as concepts related to attachment, family systems and organisational dynamics.

Above all, the term psychodynamic is used to refer to a way of understanding the meaning of human behaviour which is at all times perceived as essentially relational, dynamic and not static.

Challenging articles of faith

The pursuit of a refreshed vision for psychodynamic therapy for children and young people, whilst acknowledging the contribution of long-established psychoanalytic theory and practice, nevertheless necessitates a critical examination of this theory and practice and its historical biases. Psychotherapy trainings together with many other areas of professional endeavour that prepare students for practice, pay tribute to the works and wisdom of their founders. As the sociologist

Thomas Scheff (2003) explains, each culture (from which the scientific community is not immune) generates and reflects a variety of assumptions that are never fully declared or critically discussed, thus contributing to the maintenance of the status quo. These ruling assumptions are understood as 'tropes' which in turn give rise to a variety of linguistic and mental routines. Within child psychotherapy training as well as adult psychoanalytic training, similar sacrosanct doctrines prevail in which there is an adherence to the theories and life works of many remarkable and innovative pioneers who have made enormous contributions to our understanding of human psychology. The problem however is, that there is a serious risk that these theories, so illuminating in their time, have now become embedded and repeated as articles of faith in the various training schools. This has the potential to create an environment in which it is difficult to examine these theories critically in the light of changing circumstances, as well as for new ideas and theory to flourish.

The various embedded articles of faith also make it difficult to overturn rigid views about how psychotherapy for children should be practised. We find that what was original and innovative in the work of the pioneers of psychoanalysis with adults and children, has in some cases stagnated into doctrine. For example, the 'true gold' of child psychotherapy is almost always construed as long-term psychotherapy, sometimes over years. The further justification is that only long-term psychotherapy enables the full panoply of psychopathology to unfold. This leads us to question whether whilst we may as practitioners be fascinated by the complexity of the psychopathology; does this actually ensure that the patient gets better? In this regard, the researcher and psychotherapist Jonathan Shedler (2010) who has championed the contribution of psychodynamic psychotherapy, refers to what he describes as the preoccupation with style over content in the therapeutic discourse with respect to endlessly debating what 'really' constitutes psychotherapeutic treatment. For example, whether it is frequency of sessions or lying on the couch. In this regard Shedler reminds us that 'psychoanalysis is an interpersonal process not an anatomical position' (Shedler, 2010, p.9). In his examination of the scientific evidence to support the efficacy of psychodynamic psychotherapy (2010), Shedler makes the point that the earlier resistance to disseminate this evidence in contemporary research circles, is connected at least in part in the United States, to past 'psychoanalytic arrogance and authority' of the hierarchical exclusive medical establishment. This has played a part in creating a negative view of psychodynamic thinking amongst many mental health professionals who have gone on instead to embrace the promise of cognitive behavioural therapies. Psychoanalyst Otto Kernberg

(2014) goes further in his critical assessment of what he describes as the 'underlying authoritarian structure of psychoanalytic education' which he states has infantilised candidates, whilst creating a self-protective isolation from ideas that present alternative views and positions.

Why should psychotherapy with children and young people be long term?

A problem that confounds traditionally practised child psychotherapy is that through its adherence to the primacy of long-term work, practice becomes bound and defined by length of treatment, rather than by what actually constitutes the aims and objectives of the therapy. One of the main arguments presented in this book is that by primarily identifying child psychotherapy solely with length of treatment, we confuse method, objectives and outcome. The claim that it is this focus on long-term work that sets child psychotherapy apart from other professions is further challenged since it is akin to the surgeon who would claim that their real skills only come to the fore in lengthy surgery. The traditional view further considers that long-term psychotherapy is particularly apposite for children and young people who are described as having 'complex problems'. This term in itself tends to be a code for children and young people who have experienced significant loss and trauma or who have been subject to abuse. A psychodynamic perspective is certainly valuable in helping us to gain insight into the impact of these problems, and one would want to ensure that these children and young people have the benefit of the best help that is available. However, again one may question whether this in itself is a sufficient justification for long-term psychotherapy, as it appears to bypass the question of what the therapy actually offers in these cases. How we might respond to these complex problems, as well as other issues that children and young people face in a different way, utilising a psychodynamic approach is at the heart of the book.

A further article of faith professed is that it is only the experience of practising long- term psychotherapy that enables practitioners to successfully carry out shorter term work. Shorter term therapy is thus always presented as the base metal versus the gold of long-term treatment. It is interesting to note that practitioners of time-limited psychodynamic psychotherapy with adults are equally exercised by these dilemmas. Lemma *et al.* (2011) in presenting their protocol of time-limited dynamic interpersonal therapy for adults, already anticipate the criticism from the psychoanalytic purists in the preface to their book. The criticisms they anticipate include charges of dilution of the psychoanalytic process to the point where time-limited psychotherapy may be accused not only of being 'a bastard offspring' but may also be accused of attempting to demolish the original 'mother church' of psychoanalysis. The authors, in creating a rebuttal to these potential challenges, go to pains to indicate that their time-limited approach in fact seeks to protect psychoanalytic thinking from increasing marginalisation, and that through its modification, seeks to adapt to the changing needs of patients and their problems, as well as to the economic and social context of contemporary health provision.

Introducing an interactive model to time-limited psychodynamic psychotherapy

The underpinning argument presented in this book, is that time-limited psychotherapy for children and young people is not, and cannot be considered as a shorter or watered-down version of traditional child psychotherapy. Instead, time-limited psychotherapy views the problems presented by the child and young person as *an opportunity* to do the internal work as well as external work differently. By so doing, it provides an integrative approach that also encompasses the key people connected with the child and young person, particularly their parents, as well as significant others.

In order to be effective therefore, a psychodynamic time-limited approach to work with children and their parents must address the *total field* that surrounds the child and include as well where necessary other involved professionals. The clinical method and technique utilised in both seeing the presenting problem as *the opportunity* and engaging with the *total field* is discussed in subsequent chapters.

Finally, this book is not intended to be used as a manual, and no manualised programme is here being proposed. The primary aim of the book is to present an approach that attempts to refresh and recalibrate how we can think about and practise time-limited psychodynamic psychotherapy with children, young people and their parents. The following chapter will refer to the history of time-limited psychodynamic psychotherapy and its original pioneering focus on work with adults.

Chapter 2

A short history of time-limited psychodynamic psychotherapy with adults

Time-limited psychodynamic psychotherapy has a well-established theoretical and research base both in the UK and the US over more than 50 years. Whilst adults have been the primary focus of this therapeutic work, there are nevertheless elements of this work that can be usefully applied in developing a conceptual framework for time-limited psychodynamic psychotherapy with children and young people.

As Allan Abbass, psychiatrist, makes clear in his review of brief psychodynamic psychotherapy (Harvard Review of Psychiatry, 2012), the evidence base for brief psychodynamic psychotherapy as an effective treatment tool is well-established. There are now over 25 published outcome studies in the field which include randomised controlled trials. Abbass further draws our attention to the effectiveness of this therapy with respect to a wide range of disorders. These include personality disorder, panic disorder, resistant and complex depression and physiologically unexplained symptoms. A subsequent meta-analysis of short-term (40 or fewer sessions) psychodynamic psychotherapy with children and young people with a range of common mental disorders, Abbass et al. (2013) suggested a tendency towards increased gains over time following the end of treatment.

The pioneers of brief psychodynamic psychotherapy Michael Balint and David Malan in the UK (Malan, 1963) and Peter Sifneos (1992), Habib Davanloo (2005) and Lester Luborsky (1984) in the United States brought their separate and individual approaches to conceptualising the scope of psychodynamic psychotherapy and its application. However, they shared a broad agreement about several key components of time-limited psychodynamic psychotherapy as follows:

- That the therapist and patient identify and agree upon the focal issue or core conflict with which they will be concerned in the course of the therapy;

- That the therapist utilises an active technique in which both engage in a dynamic dialogue and interchange;
- That issues related to childhood experience connected with attachment, separation and loss and how these are understood and resolved, are perceived as central to the therapeutic task;
- That transference interpretations are very much to the fore with respect to how the patient experiences the therapist and how this connects with their past history.

The British pioneers David Malan and Michael Balint

David Malan, psychiatrist and psychoanalyst, carried out his major research study of brief psychotherapy in 1963 under the leadership of Michael Balint, psychoanalyst. Michael Balint had already pioneered the wider application of the psychodynamic method in work with general medical practitioners described in his famous 1957 book *The Doctor, his Patient and the Illness*. Here, Balint demonstrated that the doctor–patient interaction however brief, contains within it dynamic relational elements that can be used to better understand not only the problem the patient brings, but also how the doctor responds to the problem. The *Balint groups* which emerged from this model continue to the present day. The Balint groups focus on peer group discussion with a group leader, in which the doctor participants describe their experiences of patients who may, for example, present as particularly challenging. The group discussion assists with the development of greater insight on the part of the doctor, which leads to more effective practice.

In Malan's research study of 21 therapies which took place over a period of three years, he found that it was possible to obtain long-standing improvements not only symptomatically, but also with respect to underlying neurotic behaviour patterns in patients with relatively extensive and long-standing psychological difficulties. The findings indicated that the key factors that contributed to the positive outcome were the motivation of the patient, the enthusiasm and engagement of the therapist, exploration of transference from the outset, and finally the exploration of grief and anger at termination. Malan's contention is that a basic assumption of brief psychotherapy (and possibly long-term psychotherapy), is that the therapist cannot solve all problematic areas of the patient's life. Malan similarly to the other pioneers of brief psychodynamic psychotherapy, asserted that successful therapeutic outcomes are dependent on what he referred to as 'the triangle of insight' as an inherent part of the therapeutic process. The triangle of insight reflects what is happening in the present to the patient, what is happening between the therapist and the patient, and how both relate to the past traumatic or difficult experiences of the patient.

North American pioneers of Brief Psychodynamic Psychotherapy

Malan's important findings appear to have found greater interest and response amongst American psychoanalytic psychotherapists and psychiatrists than possibly amongst his own colleagues in the UK. The mid 20th century saw a particularly fruitful exposition of ideas and research into time-limited psychodynamic psychotherapy. These North American pioneers contributed a new dimension to the research and training process through their utilisation of the then novel audio-visual resources.

Peter Sifneos

Malan's research was duplicated by Peter Sifneos (1992) at the Massachussets General Hospital in Boston in the 1960s and 1970s. Sifneos maintained that an active approach for both patient and therapist was essential to the success of time-limited psychodynamic psychotherapy. He coined the term 'Anxiety Provoking Psychotherapy' not in the sense of deliberately making the patient anxious, but in acknowledging the inevitable challenges of the psychotherapy process. For Sifneos, the willingness on the part of the patient to change, was a key selection criterion for considering which patients would be suitable for time-limited psychotherapy. A successful outcome in therapeutic terms would be reflected in the capacity of the patient to be able to 'internalise' the therapist; in other words to internalise a helpful person and process that can continue to be of use to the patient in the course of their life experience.

Habib Davanloo

Habib Davanloo (2005) working at McGill University and at Montreal General Hospital in Canada, created a large case study series of research into time-limited psychodynamic psychotherapy mainly over the 1960s and 1970s. Davanloo believed that brief psychotherapy had the potential to achieve long-term structural character change. Through the use of an active interrogative technique that intensified the therapeutic process, Davanloo sought to tackle what he perceived as patients' self-defeating behavioural and relational patterns. His empirical findings led to the recognition of the role of trauma in early attachment bonds, and the impact this has on life-long patterns of dysfunctional symptom formation. Davanloo developed what he described as a new 'metapsychology of the unconscious' in which he asserted that the role of resistance had to be carefully taken into account as a critical element in the therapeutic process. Davanloo postulated that the patient, by resisting insight, manages or lessens their anxiety at least in the short term, by deploying various defences which push their emotions back into the unconscious.

One of Davanloo's particular contributions with respect to technique in time-limited psychodynamic psychotherapy was his emphasis on the importance of the first session. The first session is perceived as not solely about fact gathering, but as critical in establishing the focus of the therapy, and from the outset interpreting the transference. Whilst the latter would be considered to be intrinsic to all psychodynamic therapy, the limited number of sessions would in themselves be a contributing factor in elevating the intensity of the transference experience.

Both Sifneos and Davanloo whilst recognising the complexity of the time-limited psychotherapeutic task which relies on the experience of the therapist, nevertheless considered the enthusiasm of the starting out psychotherapist as a positive factor in contributing to a successful outcome.

Lester Lurborsky and Supportive–Expressive Psychotherapy

Lester Luborsky (1984) was Professor of Psychology in the Department of Psychiatry at the University of Pennsylvania School of Medicine. He is particularly well-known for the manualised exposition of Supportive–Expressive Psychotherapy (SE); supportive in deriving from the supportive relationship with the therapist and expressive with respect to attempting to understand what the patient is expressing. A key element in this conceptual framework is Luborsky's identification of the Core Conflictual Relationship Theme Method (CCRT). This model has similarities to attending to the focal issue that is at the heart of all time-limited psychodynamic psychotherapy.

Luborsky attempted to identify both the timing and the process inherent in successful therapy, and how these factors are connected to the essential partnership between the therapist and patient. Luborsky posed the question that all therapists of all persuasions need to address, namely what contributes to the curative elements in psychotherapy? Luborsky's responses to this question may be summarised with respect to the particular capacities that both the patient and the therapist bring to the therapeutic endeavour as follows:

- Achieving understanding; the patient's involvement in this understanding and the therapist's ability to help the patient become involved in this task;
- The patient experiencing the relationship with the therapist as helpful and the therapist continuing to promote a helpful therapeutic experience;
- The patient's ability to internalise and hold on to the gains of treatment;
- The ability of the therapist to enable the patient to work through the ending of treatment and its meaning in a manner that enables the patient to utilise the benefits of the treatment in the longer term.

Luborsky's analysis of the patient's core relationship problems is helpful in the context of addressing what he calls the 'theme' of the patient's core relationship problems. He recommends that the therapist review what he calls 'relationship episodes' in the sessions with the patient, which offer a narrative of their interactions with other people including with the therapist. These 'narratives' in essence represent enactments in a condensed form. The therapeutic manual based on the Core Conflictual Relationship Theme Method devised by Luborsky, includes both quantitative as well as qualitative scoring, based on the transcript or process recording of the interaction between patient and therapist. By extending his conceptual framework to include ways of evaluating and scoring responses and assessing outcomes, Luborsky's work created a solid evidence base for his therapeutic method.

Contemporary approaches to time-limited psychodynamic psychotherapy with adults

In Shedler's (2010) landmark research analysis on 'The Efficacy of Psychodynamic Psychotherapy', he makes the point that effect sizes for psychodynamic psychotherapy are as large as those reported for other therapies. He refers to the study by Abbass, Hancock, Henderson and Kisely (2006) which utilised a methodologically rigorous meta-analysis of psychodynamic therapy published by the Cochrane Library. The studies which compared patients with a wide range of mental disorders (depression, anxiety, somatic symptoms) who received time-limited psychodynamic psychotherapy of 40 hours, with controls consisting of a waiting list, minimal intervention or 'treatment as usual' showed positive findings with respect to reduction of symptoms. In addition, these improvements had increased at long-term follow-up. Shedler quotes similar results of a meta-analysis (Leichsenring, Rabung and Leibing, 2004) published in the *Archives of General Psychiatry* which indicates the positive clinical results in 17 'high quality' randomised controlled trials of time-limited psychodynamic psychotherapy where the average number of sessions was 21.

However, the challenges presented by the randomised controlled trial as the gold standard of evidence-based practice, pose a particular problem for psychodynamic psychotherapy. As Shedler states, the goal of the therapy is not simply symptom remission for the patient, but the development of psychological capacities that are intrinsically associated with 'self-reflection' and 'self-discovery'. Both self-reflection and self-discovery are perceived by psychodynamic psychotherapists as contributing to long-term psychological health. These reservations are echoed by Alessandra Lemma, Mary Target and Peter Fonagy (2011) in their discussion of their model of time-limited adult psychotherapy known as Dynamic Interpersonal Therapy (DIT). They make the point that whilst evidence-based practice remains a requirement as the primary driver of contemporary healthcare, the self-limiting nature of what is deemed to be evidence does not take into account the complexity of lived experience, particularly with respect to what constitutes wellbeing.

There is further disquiet concerning the fact that the 'gold standard' of the RCT may be somewhat overvalued given the information that is increasingly coming to light about how large-scale funded studies specifically into drug treatments, are silent about their 'null findings' (Rawlins, 2008). A further factor as Lemma *et al.* point out, is that most evidence-based research does not create a space for patient participation. This in effect limits our knowledge about what is actually happening for the distressed patient and how to evaluate which treatments may contribute to their wellbeing (Dolan, 2008). In their 2011 paper Lemma *et al.* describe a pilot study involving the treatment of 16 depressed patients as a prelude to a future larger scale randomised controlled trial. In the pilot study, DIT was associated with a significant reduction in reported symptoms. The protocol developed by Lemma *et al.* (2011) is closely aligned with a set of competencies that specify the training requirements and skills required to work effectively with DIT, with the aim of creating a coherent practice manual that can be utilised by practitioners trained in psychodynamic psychotherapy. As the authors explain, their aim is not to invent a new model of psychodynamic therapy, but rather to provide a pragmatic model for time-limited psychotherapy with primarily anxious and depressed patients. The authors confirm that therapists experienced in long-term work cannot 'simply export' the techniques and framework of long-term work to time-limited therapy.

The following chapter will review some of the current research in time-limited psychotherapy with respect to children and adolescents.

Chapter 3

A critical assessment of research and outcome studies of time-limited psychodynamic psychotherapy with children and young people

Introduction

This chapter will address some of the contemporary developments with respect to research and outcome studies in time-limited psychodynamic psychotherapy with children and young people. Several key studies are discussed including 'manualised' models of time-limited psychotherapy. The challenges of fulfilling the requirements of the randomised controlled trial will be addressed, and will be followed by a critical assessment of the method and meaning of contemporary research particularly for children, parents and young people.

Psychodynamic psychotherapy particularly with respect to child and adolescent psychotherapy has come late to the area of researching its findings and creating a sense of transparency about what works for whom. It is difficult to avoid the observation that much of the current research now taking place appears to have an underlying agenda of needing to prove professional relevancy within a cost-cutting health and welfare government environment. The impact this may have on what is researched and how this research is carried out is discussed in more detail below. Nevertheless, the increasing attention to time-limited psychotherapy with children and adolescents in many of these research projects points to a recognition of the potential efficacy of short-term psychotherapeutic work.

Midgley and Kennedy (2011) who have been at the forefront of much of the current research into the efficacy of psychodynamic psychotherapy for children and young people, carried out an extensive review in which they identified 34 separate studies including nine randomised controlled trials that indicated the effectiveness of psychodynamic psychotherapy. Interestingly, of the nine randomised controlled trial studies at Level 1 of the design hierarchy for research methodology, four of these referred to time-limited psychotherapy (Trowell *et al.*, 2003; Trowell *et al.*, 2007; Trowell *et al.*, 2009; Trowell *et al.*, 2010).

Meta-analyses have yielded further useful information with respect to the efficacy of time-limited psychotherapy with children and adolescents. Abbass *et al.* (2013) conducted a meta-analysis of 11 controlled outcome studies specifically to evaluate the effectiveness of short-term psychodynamic psychotherapy for children and adolescents who presented with a wide range of common mental disorders. The 11 studies included a total of 655 patients who received 40 or fewer sessions. The review suggested that time-limited psychotherapy was effective for a range of disorders and that these gains were noticeable in follow-up. However, given the heterogeneity of the sample the authors urge some caution in interpreting the results.

Midgley and Kennedy make the important point that we need to keep in mind that '"hierarchy of evidence" does not necessarily reflect the *quality* of the study'.

Midgley (2009) has also separately addressed the vexed issue of how the randomised controlled trial forces the researcher to control for so many variables in order to make the research methodology sound, and that there is thus a risk of making the research as a whole less meaningful. In this respect he raises the question of how one assesses what kind of information counts.

The pursuit of the randomised controlled trial

The most significant recent development with respect to researching the benefits and outcomes of a time-limited psychotherapy treatment model, is the UK based IMPACT (Improving Mood with Psychoanalytic and Cognitive Therapies) study (Goodyer *et al.*, 2011).

The IMPACT study claims to be the largest comparative randomised controlled treatment trial ever carried out in Britain with a clinical population of 480 adolescents diagnosed with moderate to severe depression. The IMPACT study has taken place across three regions in the UK and in several clinic settings. The IMPACT study and treatment model utilises a manualised psychotherapy treatment programme which consists of 28 sessions for the young person and seven parent sessions. The manualised psychotherapy programme follows on the adolescent depression study initiated by Dr. Judith Trowell *et al.* (2003; 2007) and by Trowell and Miles (2011).

The full results and interpretations of data for the IMPACT study are still pending. The intention is for the research manual to become a clinical manual utilised by clinicians in child and adolescent mental health services.

However, one of the principal investigators of the trial, Professor Ian Goodyer in his presentation of the preliminary IMPACT findings to an international conference (2014), has referred to less than hoped for positive results overall, particularly with respect to rates of relapse. Goodyer's conclusions at this review, remain remarkably similar to the initial justification for the research, which is that knowledge about the particular efficacy of different psychological therapies for the treatment of adolescent depression still remain unclear.

Time-limited psychotherapy specifically with adolescents and young people appears to have become the preferred focus of much contemporary research as well as outcome studies and manualised treatments such as the IMPACT study described above. This may be due in part to a belief that adolescents and young people benefit from being seen individually. It may also, however, reflect a need on the part of researchers to find a 'neater' more contained subject for the research inquiry that is less 'contaminated' by the messiness of parental involvement, as well as other extraneous factors and this is discussed in more detail in the critical evaluation of this research.

Effective time-limited psychodynamic psychotherapy with adolescents is also described by Shefler (2000) who has adapted James Mann's (1973) model of short-term dynamic psychotherapy. This model delineates an intake period about the presenting problem and the patient's view of the problem. At the conclusion of this intake process, the therapist formulates the central issue to be explored which comprises recognition of the patient's abilities and strengths; the main emotional issues in the patient's life; and finally the self-perception of the patient. In Shefler's paper, this framework is applied to time-limited therapy with a highly motivated and articulate young adult. The Israeli context of the therapy with its focus on compulsory army service as a rite of passage whilst interesting, has contextual limitations. One would have hoped, for example, for a discussion about how the militarised nature of Israeli life may have an impact in itself, on the course of adolescence and adult identity.

A further time-limited approach to psychodynamic psychotherapy with adolescents has been designed by Briggs and Lyon (2012); Time-limited Adolescent Psychodynamic Psychotherapy (TAPP). This is a 20-session dynamic psychotherapy aimed at young people aged 14–25. The psychodynamic approach is combined with a psycho-social element and focuses on the problems associated with transitions for the young person. TAPP is a manualised therapy, with a protocol that provides a detailed guide for the clinician in order to ensure that the model is adhered to. TAPP is designed to meet the needs of young people with complex presentations including self-harm and suicidal ideation, as well as post-traumatic experiences and anxieties concerning separation. Practitioners follow a training course and must fulfil particular requirements in order to become certified to administer the therapy.

The limitations of studies on time-limited psychodynamic therapy for children and young people

A common and problematic thread that links research and outcome studies of psychotherapy for children and young people, is the fact as mentioned earlier, that the adolescent is in most cases the primary subject of study. In the research quoted above, identification of the adolescent or young person as the patient with a diagnosable mental illness or psychological/emotional difficulty lies at the core of the inquiry. This immediately takes the presenting problem out of the family and social context. We may argue that in adult psychotherapy, the adult brings themselves to therapy and takes responsibility for their problem and its treatment. Children and young people as minors however, are in a completely different situation and the psychological problems they present have significant meaning well beyond their individual selves.

When we examine the various child and adolescent outcome studies, we find that they do not perceive the interaction between the young person and their parents as being of central significance. This is both with respect to the treatment model, as well as with respect to how this model may influence outcome. Thus in the case of the IMPACT study, seven separate sessions are offered to parents versus 28 to the young person. This does not appear to be part of an interactive process. It is difficult to avoid the observation that in these research models, parents are relegated to the margins of their children's treatment as well as their experience. It may therefore not be surprising that the outcomes of these studies are less positive than they might be. The problem appears to be that the method of inquiry here unnecessarily restricted, is a more significant contributor to the research outcome, than the quality of the data gathered. The method of inquiry also replicates what is essentially an adult centric model. Regrettably, whilst the proponents of psychodynamic psychotherapy are anxious to maintain their relevance through research and outcome studies, their employment of reductionist research methodologies do not serve the task well as it leads to what may be described as a methodological entrapment.

Additionally, a research inquiry such as the IMPACT study, attempts to service a number of different agendas simultaneously, some of which are clearly not compatible. There is first the need to prove the superiority of one mode of treatment over another for depression, namely psychodynamic psychotherapy versus cognitive behavioural therapy. Second, it would appear that the professional interests of the principal investigator Goodyer (2014) lie in a completely different direction, which is that of neuroscience. This is reflected in the Study Protocol (Goodyer, 2011) which states, 'We will also determine whether time to recovery and/or relapse are moderated by variations in brain structure and function and selected genetic and hormone biomarkers taken at entry'. Thus, the design of the study required the participants additionally, to comply with submitting saliva samples for investigation of the hormone cortisol, as well as undergoing magnetic resonance imaging.

Given his reference to the disappointing initial findings of the IMPACT study, Goodyer (2014) has made it clear that he considers 'behavioural phenotyping' and ways of developing understanding of 'endocrine and neural biomarkers' through the establishment of mathematical models, the most promising approach to the treatment of adolescent depression. He concludes that this will enable practitioners to create a regime of 'personalised medicine' or a 'bespoke treatment package' for each adolescent that is bound to improve the way in which practitioners manage adolescent depression.

The question here appears to be that of incompatibility of discourses within this large research project. The fact that groups of practitioners come to the inquiry about adolescent depression from different theoretical and clinical positions is not in itself the problem. A problem emerges when there is no reflective dialogue between the proponents of these different approaches. Rather than being forced to react against each other, one would hope that this multi-centred focus could be used to constitute an inter-subjective search and inquiry into the problem of adolescent depression.

It is salutary in this respect to return to the opening paragraph of the IMPACT Study Protocol which states, 'First depressive episodes tend to arise in vulnerable individuals exposed to current chronic psychosocial adversities and acute adverse life events'. The complexity and interpersonal and systemic elements of this problem would be unlikely to come to the fore if the parameters used to measure the effectiveness of outcome of therapy are indeed set within exclusive bio-medical criteria. For example, assessing the brain scans of the adolescents will trump the changes ascribed to therapeutic intervention, since these findings cannot be so easily reduced to these measurable parameters. The complexity and meaning of the life events for the adolescents and their families further tends to recede in the light of the linear focus on outcome, negatively constructed as in 'time to recovery' and 'risk for relapse'.

It is interesting to note that Shedler (2010) makes the point that outcome studies generally fail to show differences between treatments even if significant differences do exist. Shedler's explanation for this is that there is a 'mismatch between what psychodynamic therapy aims to accomplish and what outcome studies typically measure' (Shedler, 2010, p.105). Shedler goes on to say that the primary reason for this, is that psychological health cannot be considered as the mere absence of symptoms, and that our research attention would be better focused on the 'positive presence of inner capacities and resources that allow people to live life with a greater sense of freedom and possibility' (Shedler, 2010, p.105).

Current research dilemmas in the aftermath of modernity

As mentioned earlier, child psychotherapy has come late to the field of research and to allowing for greater transparency with respect to its work and effectiveness. Given that this poses a dilemma, it would be unfortunate if in their anxiety to prove their relevance, child psychotherapists would be lured into a research methodology that inherently represents a 'modernity bias', and is therefore already dated. That is, research that is almost always concerned with trying to demonstrate how to eliminate problems *within* the individual child and adolescent. In fact this modernist position is one of espousing a de-contextualised and non-situated epistemology which is at odds with up to date research methodology in a variety of fields.

An exclusive focus on psychopathology that tries to fit the adolescent into an adultist framework, in which their pathology is separately identified without recourse to context, has severe limitations. It would also substantially limit the potential for positive outcomes. The neuro-psychologist Ray Sugarman (2004) describes this as the 'linear epistemological trap that surrounds so much of the current bio-behavioural diagnoses of the child and young person'. As Sugarman argues, the focus on the 'single causative agent' within a bio-behavioural diagnosis, asks what makes the child ill, rather than asking the question, 'Why has this child/young person produced these symptoms at this stage of his/her life?' With respect to research on adolescent depression for example, we should proceed with caution in de-coupling the adolescent from their family, either through believing that adolescents should only be seen without parental involvement, or as mentioned earlier by placing parental involvement at the margins. Ultimately, it is the critical work involved in helping the adolescent and young person make sense of their relationships within the family that will help them to make sense of themselves.

In our post-modern era, despite what appears to be the continual quest for unified standards of measurement as a kind of holy grail, we need to acknowledge that this quest is in reality one of futility. There can no longer be any single universal criterion, truth, formula or set of standards and measurement, that can be applicable across the board, particularly when this relates to psychotherapeutic practice and its outcome. The notion that researchers can devise some global grand design to encompass these issues may be understood at least to some extent as a defence against the anxiety of having to live with uncertainty. Professor Sir Michael David Rawlins (2011), Chairman of the National Institute for Health and Clinical Excellence (NICE) argues that we should be sceptical of using hierarchies of evidence where they replace the capacity for judgement, and result in evidence that is in fact 'an over-simplistic pseudo quantitative assessment of the quality of available evidence', (Rawlins, p.6). In his Harveian Oration address (2008) to the Royal College of Physicians, he states that investigators need to shift from their entrenched positions, and that hierarchies of evidence need to be 'replaced by accepting – indeed embracing – a diversity of approaches' (p.34). These above all should reflect a sophisticated capacity for judgement that is essential to the interpretation of evidence and its ultimate value.

What kind of research inquiry is helpful for the promotion of child and family wellbeing?

As described above, we would need to be wary of the linear epistemological trap of conventional RCT as the sole mode of research inquiry. Mary Target (2012), prolific researcher and psychoanalyst, warns of the illusion of believing that that which cannot be measured is unimportant or does not exist. This resonates with the view of the economist and philosopher Friedrich August von Hayek (1974) who likens this to 'perpetuating a fiction that factors that can be measured are the only ones that are relevant'. This leads, as he states, to ignoring phenomena that may appear too complex for conventional measurement, but if ignored lead to an acceptance of 'measurable' evidence for what may be a false theory.

Target has made the case for combining research methods both quantitative and qualitative, and how this combination can enrich both the therapeutic as well as the research inquiry (Target, 2012). She refers in particular to the sub-section of the IMPACT study called IMPACT ME – My Experience which will report on the experiences of a sub-group of patients focusing particularly on the meaning attributed to their depression, as well as their experience of treatment. Target also takes the view that trying to prove the relevance of psychodynamic work cannot be done solely by carrying out research, but requires engaging in discussion and debate about different types of evidence with the policy decision-makers, and those who recruit therapeutic services.

However, even here there appears to be confusion about what exactly is being represented to decision-makers; is it the psychoanalytic enterprise with its need to justify the expense involved in long-term treatment for children and young people, or is it altogether a different way of configuring a psychodynamic approach? It is interesting to note in this respect that according to Target, studies of 'psychoanalytic' child psychotherapy have not demonstrated to date the longer term improved functioning or 'sleeper effect' which has been found in studies of adult psychotherapy (Abbass et al., 2006; Leichsenring et al., 2004). This may be due at least in part to the fact that we cannot take an adult-centric approach to research on adolescent depression and expect it to give us the same results as depression in adults. A methodology that focuses primarily on individual pathology, and that does not take into account the contextual and relational experience of the young person, is bound to have limited outcomes.

Broadening the scope of time-limited psychodynamic psychotherapy

A potentially more fruitful approach to considering what we are actually asking of the therapeutic process, and how this may be assessed, is that of the broader relationship based 'mentalisation' framework developed by Mary Target, Peter Fonagy, Nick Midgley and other research psychoanalysts and therapists working out of the Anna Freud Clinic; in particular Bateman and Fonagy (2008, 2013). Ways of utilising the mentalisation framework in work with children, young people and families is described by Midgley and Vrouva (2012) as the cornerstone of therapeutic change, as it is focused on the capacity to think and reflect upon, feelings and actions of the self and others. The mentalisation framework has its foundation in attachment, developmental research and findings from neuroscience, as well as psychoanalysis. The authors refer to 'mentalising-enhancing interventions' that can be applied outside of the immediate clinical setting, for example with hard to reach adolescents. The approach can also be applied in school settings where the mentalisation approach takes a more systemic stance. For example in tackling bullying in schools, the focus is on the relationship between all the members in the school rather than on simply identifying the 'culprits'.

A promising approach to working with adolescents with complex mental health needs that uses Adolescent Mentalisation-Based Integrative Therapy (AMBIT) is described by Bevington et al. (2013).

Mentalisation in this context is used as an 'organising framework' where a number of 'multiple modalities' both with respect to care for the young person, as well as support for the network, are contained within a single worker. This approach places a particular emphasis on preventing the breakdown not only of the young person, but also of the key professional relationships that surround the young person.

Finally, broadening the scope of time-limited therapeutic intervention has also been shown to be effective at the other end of the age range in work with under-fives. Whilst not officially part of a research study, the usefulness of a parent inclusive approach is demonstrated in the long-standing Tavistock Clinic Under-Fives Counselling Service. This service has gone from strength to strength in demonstrating the considerable capacity for change and positive outcome following a brief psychotherapeutic intervention of usually five sessions. Maria Pozzi (2003) in her detailed account of the work of the Under-Fives Counselling Service, describes how it benefits from an amalgam of a psychoanalytic as well as a systemic framework, which succeeds in bringing the presenting problems and their history, into the 'here and now' of the sessions so that they can be contained and understood.

In the context of this therapeutic work with under-fives, Pozzi-Monzo, Lee and Likierman (2012) carried out research that involved clinical description and quantitative data, drawn from videotaped clinical material. The results demonstrated a significant lessening of the presenting symptoms, albeit with a small sample of families.

Psychodynamic psychotherapy with children and young people at a crossroads

The account of the research and the findings indicate that psychodynamic therapy and its application within publicly funded services is at a crossroads. As discussed in this chapter, the move to prove efficacy and relevance of psychodynamic psychotherapy with children and young people, via the randomised controlled trial may not only be considered inappropriate but also outdated. Mary Target (2012) in an address to the British Psychoanalytical Society Research Lecture has described the prejudice concerning psychodynamic research amongst those bodies responsible for research funding. These funding bodies tend to take the position that no amount of evidence can ever justify a psychodynamic approach (Troupp and Catty, 2012). This may lead us to question why we persist with trying to force our way through a door that appears to remain so resolutely closed. How can this be in the real interests of the people we are trying to help, namely children, parents and families?

A different line of approach is needed, in which the focus of our efforts more appropriately shifts to that of primary prevention. Read and Bentall (2012) for example, in their paper on the impact of negative childhood experiences, make the point that the mental health professions have been slow, as well as reluctant, to acknowledge the role of childhood adversity and its impact on future psychiatric and social disorders. Read and Bentall advocate that the most effective way to ameliorate this problem is to put our energies into primary prevention, exploring the causes of these problems within a broader psychological and social context. This view is supported in further studies on the impact of adverse childhood experiences on adult health behaviours and outcomes (Bentall *et al.,* 2012; Bellis *et al.,* 2014). The following chapter will make a case for the recalibration of the psychodynamic enterprise as a whole, and for a re-evaluation and valuing of what this approach has to offer to children, young people, parents and families, both with respect to therapeutic intervention as well as to this broader objective of child, adolescent and family wellbeing.

Part 2

A conceptual and practice framework for time-limited psychodynamic psychotherapy with children, young people and parents

Chapter 4

Reconfiguring a psychodynamic approach for current times

Refreshing and redefining the psychodynamic enterprise

The four domains as cornerstones in time-limited psychotherapy with children, young people and their parents

It is proposed that we need to refresh and redefine the psychodynamic enterprise for our current times, particularly with respect to how we configure time-limited psychotherapy with children, young people and their parents. This necessarily involves reconfiguring some of the foundations of our clinical intervention moving away from an exclusively individual and linear approach, to one that is integrative and interactive. In order to do so, we need to attend simultaneously to four different but interconnected domains within the therapeutic encounter. These domains are identified as follows:

- **The intra-psychic:** The internal experience of the child, young person and their parents. What the presenting behaviour 'means'.
- **The inter-personal:** What takes place between the child, the young person and their parents.
- **The systemic:** What takes place within the family system. How the child and young person 'speak' the family.
- **The environmental:** The impact of the living arrangements that surround the child and young person, such as school, childcare and broader social and cultural factors.

These four interconnected domains represent the real space, time and experience that children, young people and their parents actually inhabit and that cannot be kept artificially separate from each other within the therapeutic encounter. For this reason alone, a psychodynamic perspective encompassing as it does these four domains is perceived as providing a particularly apposite conceptual and clinical framework. In much of clinical practice however, these domains are kept separate from each other, often resulting in varying degrees of fragmentation. In other words, an integrated position that acknowledges the interconnectedness of the four domains, is the opposite of a position in which practitioners avoid contact with parents, or with significant others connected with the child, because they believe that they must preserve the 'purity' of approach in individual therapy with a child or young person.

A further problem that emerges in this connection is the tendency to refer to everything as 'psychoanalytic' that pertains to a non-behavioural deeper, meaning-making approach, whether this refers to therapy with individuals, families or groups. This generic usage inevitably raises confusion with respect to treatment versus method and also denies the contribution of systems thinking and understanding of group dynamics, which while it is a part of a psychodynamic way of thinking, is not psychoanalysis. If we are to be able to provide clarity on these matters, then we must ensure that the order of words does not become the order of things (Good and Kleinman, 1985). For this reason, the acknowledgment of the four domains needs to become integrated within the mind of the therapist as well as within their clinical practice.

Commencing with widening the field as part of the therapeutic endeavour

The point has been made earlier that the framework within which we currently conduct treatment for children and young people, as well as the accompanying research, is too narrowly circumscribed. In addition, when this framework is predicated on the identification of psychopathology then we have already foreclosed on the problem. By taking the four domains as a cornerstone of all clinical practice and intervention, we create a widening of the field of inquiry that will enable us to more accurately identify the problem and find more meaningful solutions. Further, by widening the field of inquiry and encompassing *the total field* that surrounds the child and young person, the therapeutic process is able to have a greater impact over a relatively shorter period of time. Thus the total field surrounding the child and young person is perceived as being part of a complex dynamic system of which the components may all require attention at various times.

Our work as psychotherapists is to address the tension and interplay between these different domains at different points or stages in the therapy. Therefore, we may at one point in the therapy address an internalised struggle for the child, and at another time communicate with parents, or with a teacher about the child. Underlying this process is the recognition that all of these interactions are perceived as having similar therapeutic 'value' in the service of helping the child and young person. An image that comes to mind is that of a glass prism which is made up of similar, equal and parallel ends. Different parts of the prism when held up to the light will reflect different colours of the rainbow.

Attending to the different elements of the field surrounding the child and young person, is best carried out by the same therapist rather than allocated to different people, because the therapist needs to be able to make it credible and workable. This resonates with the approach referred to earlier of Bevington *et al.* (2013). By widening the field of the total therapeutic enterprise, the therapist contains the function of case manager as well as that of therapist at various times. Both are perceived as having equal therapeutic value, and as complementing each other in attending to the needs of the child and young person.

This approach is illustrated in the following example. A therapist working with a young child in permanent foster care was aware of the impact of her early difficult experience, particularly with respect to her fear of loss and separation. The therapist was informed by the foster parents that she was having difficulties at her kindergarten, where the teacher continually complained about her challenging behaviour. Here, we might draw an initial conclusion that the child's traumatic early history was a contributing factor to her behavioural problems. Whilst this was not incorrect, it only presented a partial picture. The therapist resolved to visit the kindergarten to speak to the teacher and suggest ways in which they could both work towards helping the child. At the visit, the therapist found an older, very harassed, woman in charge, who was clearly no longer enjoying the job of caring for any of the children, let alone the little girl in question. She was dismissive of the therapist, and reluctant to engage in any discussion about ways of helping the child, preferring to see her as 'the problem'.

The accumulation of data as described in this example that follows from a widening of the field, and which accompanies the therapy of the child and parents, is of considerable benefit in helping us not to jump to conclusions about a problem. It also assists us with respect to not taking premature or incorrect action before we have more of the total picture. By the same token, a school or kindergarten visit can reveal supportive and engaged staff who bring their own insight to bear on the problem, and through this collaborative experience, contribute to the containing holding function that can be so critical for children and young people.

The issue of confidentiality when the therapy is contained within a single worker is often cited in these situations to justify why such an approach may not be appropriate. However, whilst we need to take a protective and confidential approach where required, we also need to be vigilant about a slavish adherence to confidentiality which may be used as a defence to justify a lack of communication with parents and caregivers, as well as with other professionals. In fact, clinical experience indicates that children and young people have a great longing to be understood by their parents; in many cases they want the psychotherapist to be able to 'hold' the whole picture of the important people in their lives.

The attention to the total field surrounding the child and young person inevitably changes, expands and contracts at different times depending on the presenting problem, and requires an evaluation of what may be the appropriate 'leverage' at any point in time to effect positive change. Encompassing the total field of the child and young person's experience has the further function of reducing fragmentation. It also provides a model for a way of thinking about, and understanding of, the problem that can be readily accessed by parents and caregivers. In this sense the ability of the psychotherapist to hold in mind these different fields promotes both integration and containment. There may of course be occasions in clinical settings where it is strongly indicated that two practitioners work together, for example in high-risk situations.

When two practitioners work together, it is imperative that they share the same conceptual understanding and method of working. Where this does not take place and where the emphasis instead is on 'dividing up' the problem, or 'dividing up' the child, this will almost always result in a poor outcome.

Recalibrating the psychodynamic enterprise

Working within the framework of the four domains enables us to recalibrate the psychodynamic enterprise, as it takes into account the broad scope of psychodynamic influence not only with respect to individual development and experience, but also with respect to our understanding of family systems, organisational life, culture and community. Psychodynamic clinical and research experience already encompasses all of these elements and provides the connecting thread between the four domains described above. Over the 20th century, the psychodynamic enterprise has provided valuable information and expertise with respect to the following key areas concerned with child and family wellbeing. These are:

1   The importance of the child–parent relationship that provides the building blocks for life and emotional wellbeing.
2   The impact of early life experience, particularly trauma in early childhood and adolescence.
3   The centrality of meaning making and the sharing of meaning as an intrinsic component of all human interaction.

Psychodynamic thinking and practice have made practical and unique contributions in all three areas, and by so doing, has contributed significantly to improving outcomes for children, young people, parents and families. For example, clinical and research evidence on the importance of attachment for young children has revolutionised the way we view early childhood services, and children experiencing separation and loss; utilising infant observational techniques combined with understanding of early infancy has made significant contributions to infant/parent mental health; taking a family systems approach has enhanced our understanding of the complexity of family dynamics and taking a psychodynamic perspective of groups and organisations has enabled services to recover and renew themselves in the light of changing circumstances.

Above all a psychodynamic approach acknowledges *a line of continuity* between the inner world of the child, interpersonal and family relationships and connections to the outside world. Central to this integrated perspective is the recognition that all behaviour has meaning, and is a communication. Additionally, behaviour rather than being perceived as rigid and fixed, is at all times perceived as dynamic and constantly changing. However, whilst there have been some connections in the past between the proponents of these different elements of the psychodynamic enterprise, it is evident that these have been insufficient, perhaps due to professional rivalry, or timidity to withstand and counter the criticism from the reductionist bio-behaviourists. As a result, in recent years the influence of the psychodynamic method and thinking has waned. What is proposed here is a broad integrated approach in which the theory and practice associated with each of the domains connected to the intra-psychic, interpersonal, systemic and organisational, is perceived as all of one piece in clinical work with children, young people and parents. This gives impetus to a renewed and refreshed vision for understanding and working with the problems of children, young people and their parents, within the context of an emotional ecology. By integrating these different interconnected domains, we recalibrate the psychodynamic enterprise and instate it as a veritable powerhouse of information, research and clinical experience. This not only has relevance for the treatment of children and young people, but also for the way in which we think about childhood, adolescence, and parenthood within a much wider preventative and societal context.

The primacy of the developmental task

It has been stated earlier, that assessment and therapeutic communication with children, young people and their parents does not commence with the uncovering of pathology, but with the understanding of the meaning of their behaviour. An essential component of the psychodynamic conceptual and treatment framework therefore, is that it assumes a continuity of process and meaning, and thereby a continuity between brain and mind. This necessitates having a firm grasp of what is developmentally appropriate behaviour for the child and young person. A focus on what constitutes *the developmental task* in terms of the age and stage and what requires to be negotiated for the child and young person, is an essential requirement of any assessment process. A consideration of what may be described as the *emotional milestones of development* (Schmidt Neven, 1996, 2010) also enables us to identify what constitutes the *unifying developmental experiences* for all children and all young people, rather than what sets them apart from each other. The assertion of a unifying developmental experience for children and young people in turn, helps us to avoid fragmentation and instead to assert a set of unifying principles to inform practice.

Restating the duty of care to children young people and their parents

By recalibrating the psychodynamic approach, we move away from an individual problem-based approach, towards an interactive therapeutic model that provides the opportunity to explore the meaning of behaviour by integrating the intra-psychic, the interpersonal and the systemic domains. This model takes as its starting point that the professional's duty of care with respect to the behaviour of the child and young person in the first instance, is always to uncover meaning and context. Further, professionals have a duty of care to parents and caregivers. This recognises that the most enduring therapeutic outcomes involve not only a shift or change in the child or young person, but also an essential shift in the parents' perspective of themselves. We also need to recognise that at the societal level, parents and families as well as professionals struggle to negotiate the white water of rapid social change. Contemporary families are constituted as never before in a variety of different ways with respect to parenting and child rearing, and there is always a time lag between how people configure their lives and the services that try to catch up with them. In addition, the great beast of technology has transformed the way many of us live in the West providing us with apparent limitless opportunities, but also intruding into areas of our lives that need protection and privacy.

Psychodynamic signposts in therapeutic work: How theory and practice converge

The following section will summarise the essential elements of psychodynamic understanding that underpin the assessment and treatment process in time-limited psychotherapy with children, young people and their parents. Whilst reference is made to several important theorists and clinicians, the framework below is not intended to reflect a particular psychodynamic approach or theory. The assumption is made that by the 21st century, we have reached a point of understanding and integration of the various clinical and theoretical foundations of the psychodynamic approach. Therefore a presentation on the efficacy of time-limited psychotherapy does not have to declare its allegiance for example, as Kleinian or Freudian, or following exclusively any other theory or theoretical position. This would be rather like scientists having to reiterate their allegiance to Darwin or Newton each time they present a new finding in their work. A further assumption made, is that readers will come to the practice of time-limited psychotherapy with children, young people and parents with some background both in theoretical understanding and clinical practice.

In re-calibrating the psychodynamic enterprise, the following conceptual and therapeutic frameworks are viewed as central to time-limited psychotherapeutic practice with children, parents and families:

• Understanding the impact of attachment;
• Understanding family dynamics;
• Attending to the making of meaning and the unity of brain and mind;
• Acknowledging the capacity for health and growth in children and young people;
• Understanding group and organisation dynamics in creating a network and professional links.

Attachment: The connecting thread between the individual and systems theory

The psychodynamic inquiry concerning attachment contains within it social, emotional, cognitive and behavioural elements that form the basis of Bowlby's (1973a, 1973b, 1973c) works on Attachment, Separation and Loss. Bowlby's theory of attachment is based on the recognition of how the affectional bonds between children and their caregivers have a biological basis related to the need for the survival of the infant. The concept of an *internal working model* that is central to the theory of attachment is also central to the capacity to ascribe meaning to experience and events. Attachment is not perceived as a 'stage' of development to be outgrown, but rather as a developmental process that endures throughout the lifespan and undergoes transformation over time. It is interesting to note that whilst focusing on the individual infant, attachment theory already has strong systemic elements. The infant and caregiver are part of the same system in which they are inextricably linked to each other through the context of their interactive activity (Bowlby, 1988).

Interestingly, Bowlby had written one of the first papers on family therapy as early as 1949 in which he used family therapy sessions to accompany individual therapy with a child that had reached an impasse (Bowlby, 1949). Family therapist John Byng-Hall (1991) has discussed the particular contribution of attachment theory to family systems thinking with respect to recognising how the whole setting of family therapy can be said to provide a secure base for the family. By so doing, the secure base can be used as a model by the family to continue their exploration of their problems once the therapy is concluded. Contemporary research on attachment highlights this process in relation to emotion regulation, information processing, psychobiology and culture. Attachment is perceived as giving rise to the capacity for self-organisation in the infant and young child. This capacity for emotional regulation utilises a dynamic systems theory that reflects an interdependence of system elements that in turn give rise to new behavioural forms (Goldberg, 2000; Powell *et al.*, 2014).

The contribution of family therapy and systems thinking

The tendency for contemporary child and family mental health services to identify a problem 'within' the child is a far cry from the work of family therapy and systems theory that emerged amidst high hopes in the latter half of the last century (Ackerman, 1966; Minuchin, 1974; Satir, 1967; Skynner,1996). One of the fundamental tenets of systems theory is that it is not possible to create change in one aspect of a system, without this affecting change in another part of the system. The family system is thus conceptualised as an organisation of interdependent parts (Bateson, 1973; Watzlawick *et al.*, 1967). However, in contrast to this, when the child or young person's behaviour is viewed solely outside the dynamic of the family system, then their behaviour can be more easily categorised and reduced to a set of discretely isolated functions. These in turn can then be measured and separately analysed, without any reference to their component parts.

The fundamental tenet of family therapy as Bateson put it is that 'individuals are contextually located', and this has significant implications for the way in which we view the problems that appear to reside within the child or adolescent. The idea of context is further extrapolated by David Campbell (2003) who states that, 'without context there is no meaning'. Meaning formulation as an intrinsic element of family therapy is concerned with the relationships between members of the family. The presenting symptom of the child and young person is thus perceived as having a very specific function with respect to the family dynamic, for example with respect to maintaining family homeostasis or family regulation (Burck *et al.*, 2013).

In the subsequent chapters, clinical examples will illustrate how the symptom produced by the child and young person represents *the opportunity* for understanding the problem, rather than needing to be disposed of, since it is these symptoms, that literally 'speak the family'.

We may postulate that where there is an individual, the family is not far behind and vice versa. The presenting symptom of the child and young person may therefore be understood as having a regulatory function for the family, which is similar to the function of individual defences. The connection between individual and family or the intrapsychic and the systemic is beautifully illustrated for example in the work of the Milan school of family therapy (Selvini-Palazzoli *et al.*, 1978). Here relationship-centred questions that pose a paradoxical injunction concerning the symptom, effectively name the accompanying unconscious motivation that perpetuates the symptom.

The making of meaning and the unity of brain and mind

There is clear evidence that the capacities for emotional reciprocity and shared meaning between the infant, young child and caregivers are elicited at prime times in the early developmental period. The conclusions drawn from the research and clinical evidence, is that it is the attunement and attention of caregivers that contributes to the child's capacity for self-regulation, the absence of which appears to underlie so many of the psychological problems presented by children and young people. The psychodynamic perspective helps us to understand that shared meaning in the early infant and young child/parent relationship, not only creates a context for brain development, but also has an impact on the way the brain is wired (Schore, 1994, 2012).

Despite the extensive literature on context and meaning and its importance in early child development, this is not acknowledged in much of current clinical practice. Instead, it is the split between brain and mind more than any other area, that has come to epitomise the split between the bio-behavioural discourse and a mechanistic view of child and adolescent behaviour, versus a view that acknowledges that cognitive and other behaviours arise out of complex relational meaning-making processes.

The mechanistic view of child and adolescent behaviour has been described earlier as a 'linear epistemological trap' (Sugarman, 2004). In this respect Sugarman points out that the sole consideration of medical and other linear models with respect to understanding child and adolescent behaviour, is limited to producing what may be described as little more than 'punctuation points' in a complex system.

Recognising the capacity for health and growth in the child and young person

At the beginning of the 20th century, John Dewey, the philosopher and educationalist, introduced a dynamic and promising view of childhood that had as its central tenet the developmental understanding of children. In his presidential address to the American Psychological Association in 1899, Dewey compared children with adults, and stressed the difference between the two by defining the child as 'primarily one whose calling is growth' (Dewey cited in Sarason, 1981, p.124). However, it is often this very dynamic concerning growth and all that is implied which is missing from many of the current medicalised and pathologised diagnoses of children and young people.

It is salutary in this respect to be reminded of the extraordinary therapeutic legacy of Donald Winnicott, paediatrician and psychoanalyst, who, in his many writings can be described as the real pioneer of time-limited psychodynamic psychotherapy with children, parents and young people (1958, 1964, 1965). The child psychotherapist Christopher Reeves (2003) refers to Winnicott's reflection that he had become more convinced by 'the natural capacities for growth and self-healing in the child, given the right environmental provision, and less convinced of the indispensability of full-scale child analysis'. Winnicott conceptualised this in terms of an 'economics of therapy' not in the sense of economising or rationalising, but at the deepest level of promoting what fits the child and the child within the family.

Winnicott had further recognised over his long career, that many of the presenting problems in the child represent 'a latent displaced expression of parental states' (Reeves, 2003). Edwards and Maltby (1998) support this view by pointing to how much can be achieved in short-term focused work with children and their families 'where the unconscious itself can be "surprised" without lengthy interventions'.

They comment on how an interactive parent inclusive approach removes the burden from the child or young person of being the nominated patient. This is a factor that in itself may be worth taking into account, when we consider the disappointing results of research and outcome studies that make the presenting problem of the child or young person the primary focus.

Winnicott could be said to have already recalibrated the psychodynamic approach through his recognition of the continuity between inner and outer experience. Most importantly, his therapeutic insights acknowledge the inherent capacities within the child for growth and self-healing, as well as his conviction of the need to understand the child as living within the family and social surround. Further commentary on the Winnicottian perspective is provided by Lanyado (1996) who refers to his attention to widening the frame of the therapist's involvement with the child and young person, whether this refers to working with parents, family members, schools or other networks concerned with the child and young person. As Lanyado puts it, for Winnicott this would all be part of what is both appropriate and necessary at various times in the course of a therapy in order to maintain the 'facilitating environment' for the patient and promote effective treatment.

The psychodynamic perspective on groups and organisations

The psychodynamic perspective on groups and organisations brings a wealth of understanding and analysis of group and organisational dynamics. The pioneering work of Wilfred Bion (1962) on basic assumption groups, and Menzies-Lyth (1988, 1989) on how social systems construct defences against anxiety, is particularly relevant to the problems of fragmentation that permeate many of the organisational settings connected with the provision of contemporary child and family mental health services. In this respect the individual is at the mercy of the organisation, and the kind of treatment or service that may be finding favour at a particular time. Given the prevalence of economic constraint, contemporary organisations of every type are undergoing increasing scrutiny and review. This in itself is not necessarily a problem, but becomes so when professionals resort to defensive and formulaic modes of interpreting the behaviour of children and young people. The elevation of a technocratic managerialism is an example of a defensive response that has little to do with promoting mental health. Within technocratic managerialism, elements such as goal setting, and performance appraisal, outputs and throughputs become set in concrete as objectives in themselves. These override the original objectives of the organisation and by so doing, override the needs of the children, parents and families they have been set up to help. Krantz and Gilmore's seminal 1990 paper on this topic makes the point that the organisation, by pinning all of its hopes on the imaginary powers of management systems, serves to divert the members of the organisation from the challenges, as well as the responsibilities of their task.

How these challenges are met at the organisational and systemic level, unfortunately play out a familiar theme which is to either retreat into history, or go through a restructuring process. A sense of helplessness in the face of rapid change at the organisational level, is reflected with depressing monotony in the restructuring of programmes, services and organisations which more often than not emerge as a newly dressed up version of what has gone before; everything changes and everything remains the same.

Why more than ever, we need a psychodynamic perspective on child adolescent and family mental health problems

The prevalence of fragmentation in child and family mental health, at the level of system and structure, as well as at the level of process and function, lead to professional confusions, collusions and entanglements. This is problematic on two counts: first, it references out of date and in some cases discredited views of how children develop and how families function; second, it leads to clinical and research projects into children's psychological problems that are limited and over circumscribed. The outcome as mentioned earlier, is an increasingly depleted and impoverished discourse of childhood and parenthood, as well as a thinly disguised blame discourse about the need to find solutions that will 'crack' the problems that remain so persistently intransigent.

How has this situation come about? One explanation is that within the domain of child and family mental health, it appears overall that ways of knowing that are informed by a commitment to the search for meaning, have become silenced and marginalised within current professional practice and discourse. The marginalising of knowledge and insightful meaning tends to lead to the marginalising and fragmenting of knowledge about the child's individual psychology and the child's relationship with parents and the family. This marginalising of knowledge also inhibits the ability of children, parents and young people themselves, to reflect on, and act on, their own inherent knowledge in order to create change in their lives.

The richness of a psychodynamic method that integrates the intra-psychic, inter-personal and systemic domains has the potential to lead to an interactive therapeutic model that is in tune with the continuity between inner and outer experience for the child and young person. It is also in tune with the essential interrelationship between children, young people and their parents. It has the further function of being able to harness the essential capacities of all the parties concerned, professionals as well as patients, and to empower them to bring these capacities and strengths to the therapeutic process. How psychodynamics in action can be brought to bear on time-limited psychotherapy with children, parents and young people will be described in the following chapters.

Chapter 5

The clinical method in time-limited psychodynamic psychotherapy with children, young people and parents

In this chapter, three core elements of the approach to time-limited psychodynamic therapy with children, parents and young people are described. These are:

1   Asserting the legitimacy of the psychodynamic method and the making of meaning.
2   Attending to the developmental scaffold and the core developmental task.
3   Involving parents and caregivers in the therapeutic process.

Asserting the legitimacy of the psychodynamic method and the making of meaning

Shedler (2006) describes the great insight that the psychodynamic approach offers practitioners and patients alike, in that it 'has contributed a vocabulary with which to talk about inner contradictions and techniques for working with contradictions in ways that can alleviate suffering' (Shedler, 2006, p.14). In this regard, discovering an *emotional vocabulary* and *finding one's own voice* are the essential components both of the therapeutic process and outcome. As described in this and the following chapters, the vocabulary that is discovered is necessarily that of a shared vocabulary about behaviour, that involves children, young people and their parents and caregivers together, as far as this is possible. It is striking in the child and adolescent mental health field, how often practitioners rush straight into a proposal of psychotherapy of whatever school, before they have had a chance to ascertain the child and parents' readiness for such an intervention.

It is suggested that practitioners from the outset, are open and clarifying with patients about a psychodynamic way of working and its benefits. In a world where many parents understandably look for relief of symptoms, by being told what to do, or getting advice a mouse click away, it is easy for practitioners to get drawn into a symptom disposal mindset, rather than one in which the symptom becomes the opportunity for exploration and meaningful understanding. Creating a more transparent attitude requires that some of the 'working machinery' of the psychodynamic process, and how the practitioner arrives at a particular observation, is shared with parents. This is the opposite of maintaining a mystifying or aloof presence with respect to the therapist's professional background and way of working. A more open approach may take the form of explaining to parents that giving advice and strategies has its limitations. Strategies do not help us to understand the meaning of behaviour, because the parent will not be speaking with their own 'voice' but with the instructional voice of the therapist. Given that behaviour constantly changes, and is dynamic, we may also advise that a strategy will have a 'use by date' as it leaves our lips.

Another way of describing this open approach is to perceive it as creating the capacity for psychological mindedness in both the parents and the child and young person.

Supporting psychological mindedness in parents

Creating a setting for psychological mindedness is described in the following example, which also demonstrates how parents can be drawn into psychodynamic understanding that befits the presenting problem. A caring couple contacted the therapist requesting help for their seven-year-old son whose behaviour they found both challenging and defiant. He was described as being different from their other children, who they felt were more reasonable and compliant. They had previously seen a psychologist whose attempts to take a purely management approach to the problems had not been successful. The child's behaviour improved briefly but then reverted back to the old problems. The parents also described hypersensitivity on the part of their little boy with respect to clothing and his appearance. The therapist noted that the parents whilst caring, spoke about their life at home in very pragmatic terms, and commented that all their children had to fit into a busy family schedule. This busyness seemed to be echoed in the way the mother spoke, which had an almost rapid fire quality to it, as though she believed she was perpetually short of time. Father's reaction to the stress was to use reassurance for his son, assuring him that he was fine and much loved.

In the course of taking a history of the child, it emerged that he had suffered from a significant hearing loss which unfortunately had not been diagnosed until he was over two and a half years old. The parents reported their puzzlement that they could not understand why their son, when he was a baby, would keep his back to them when they spoke to him. They had interpreted this as the beginning of his challenging behaviour towards them. Surprisingly, the hearing loss had not been picked up by the previous psychologist and was not mentioned by the referring doctor. On seeing the child, the therapist noted an attractive little boy who was clearly using lip reading as well as listening. He tried hard to ingratiate himself with her, asking her about her children and what they were like, and focused on her clothes and jewellery. The intensity of his questioning appeared to be a way of distracting from any discussion of the problem and his fear of criticism. It became evident that the child's hearing problem had played a significant part in compromising both his capacity for attachment as well as his mother's ability to bond with him, as she had found him so difficult from the start. The therapist drew attention to the hearing problem, and made this, and the likelihood of how the hearing loss had affected the child's attachment and the mother's bonding, the central focus of the therapeutic encounter.

Helping the parents to shift from a behavioural problem focus to one in which they could begin to understand the role of attachment and bonding, and how this had been compromised by their child's hearing problem, meant that they could access not only underlying meaning, but also important knowledge of which they had been previously unaware. Once this understanding and context was established it became more appropriate to explore how they could manage the child's anxieties and some of his outbursts differently. By demonstrating child–parent interconnectedness, it helped the parents additionally to see how their child's hearing loss was also their loss. Whilst this aroused sadness in them, it also set the scene for the beginning of a more appropriate reflective process on their part, which would serve them well in the future.

Attending to the developmental scaffold and the core developmental task

Helping parents to become developmentally aware is another aspect of helping them to become psychologically minded. Identifying and promoting the developmental task for children and young people is central to the therapeutic enterprise, and it is here that time-limited psychotherapy can truly come into its own. As Rawson (2002) puts it, the primary objective of time-limited psychodynamic psychotherapy is to 'facilitate change by dealing satisfactorily with the strategic focal issue that is holding up development'. Thus, when working with children and young people, the presenting problem is always understood in the context of the developmental task. In other words, how does the child present in terms of their age and stage, related to expected social and emotional milestones? The great benefit of working with children and young people is that we are fortunate in having growth on our side. Development as Winnicott has indicated in all of his writings contains within itself the power for growth and change. This is a formidable ally in the therapeutic task. This means that the therapeutic process does not have to involve the therapist in doing all the work, but rather on helping to elicit and promote the inherent capacities within the child as well as the young person.

It may be suggested therefore that less in therapeutic practice terms becomes more. This resonates with Winnicott's contention that in work with children and young people we may want to consider how little needs to be done, before rushing into action. This process has its parallel in infant–parent relationships, as in when parents' anxiety is contained, they are able to elicit from the infant what already exists in potential and what Daniel Stern has called the infant's 'formidable capacity' (Stern, 1977).

There are many instances across the age range from early childhood through to late adolescence, in which a variety of often complex factors interrupt developmental milestones, or where they may fail to develop altogether. In one such case, a little girl of three and a half was referred because of her challenging and omnipotent behaviour within the home. There had been some physical problems at birth and postnatally and these had been resolved, but a high level of parental anxiety remained about the fragile nature of the child. The parents believed that their little girl was unusually gifted intellectually and they poured a lot of attention into stimulating learning experiences for her. However, when the therapist saw the child she felt that she was in fact surprisingly immature in terms of the abilities one might reasonably expect of her age. She was more interested in 'dazzling' the therapist with her charm and verbal ability than doing a drawing, or showing any interest in the toys. Her capacity for concentration was also limited and she had a low boredom threshold. In this case the parents had wondered if their child might be showing early signs of a disorder, but it was the therapist's belief that the rarified atmosphere surrounding the little girl and her parents' over-investment in her, were what in Rawson's terms was 'holding up development'. We may hypothesise that the child was also confused about her position in the family hierarchy; as the much admired and highly invested child, was she in fact one of the adults or one of the children? Certainly her omnipotent and highly controlling manner suggested that she believed the former might be the case. The central focus in this therapy therefore was on helping her parents create appropriate opportunities for maturation that would be child-centred and not adult-centric. Helping the parents to set firmer boundaries and be clearer about their own relationship as a couple, and as a parenting team, would also set the scene for more positive change. In this situation a visit to the childcare centre or kindergarten, was also indicated, as the little girl ostensibly had no interest in other children, but spent most of her time relating to the adults. Here we see another example of widening the field in order to get the best outcome, and ensure that all the people surrounding the child have a shared commitment to positive change.

Adhering to unifying principles of child and adolescent development

In situations where children may have diagnosable disorders such as on the autism spectrum, the core developmental task should not be lost sight of, since we are concerned with unifying principles of development, rather than what sets children and young people apart from each other. This comes particularly to the fore in working with children who have such diagnoses, where it is important not to become blinded by the symptom. Children who have obsessive behaviours, or high levels of anxiety, need to be able to live within their families, go to school and maintain relationships with peers where possible. An approach that works towards normalisation in the form of raising expectations for both the child and the parents can be useful. Many parents in these situations become encapsulated into the fearful inner world of the child and trapped there with the child. Whilst not denying the child's difficulties, a focus on the developmental task enables us to support parents to *normalise development* for the child wherever possible. This in turn normalises the parenting task and gives parents permission to set more appropriate limits and boundaries without continual recourse to making allowances for the 'disorder'.

At the opposite end of the age spectrum we meet adolescents who are struggling to find a sense of identity and are fearful of entertaining the idea of a life that does not include a lifeline to a significant parent whether father or mother. Here we may be dealing with a situation in which parents have come to believe that their adolescent boy or girl is devoid of inner resources. As a result, the parent is always called upon to clear the path. In one such example, a 15-year-old boy reflected that a group of parents had acted prematurely by rushing in to try to deal with a conflict that had arisen in his friendship group. We can see how in these situations, the wish on the part of the parents to be helpful can override and undermine the innate capacities of the children and young people themselves to address the difficulties. Helping with the developmental task of assisting the young person to move into independence therefore, also involves helping parents to manage this transition.

When we consider some of the current research on adolescent depression, there appears to be a growing assumption that adolescents represent an almost separate category, or clinical group that can be treated as though detached from their parents. However, clinical experience suggests that we should proceed with caution when it comes to de-coupling the adolescent from their family context. While it may be helpful for adolescents and young people to have therapy in their own right, it should not automatically follow that parents should be nowhere involved. The idea of the independent adolescent or young person may represent a neat subgroup for research purposes, but we need to keep in mind that it is the critical work involved in helping them through this period of transition that needs to come to the fore. This involves helping both the young person and their parents make sense of their relationships through this period of change. There are two important factors to be taken into account in working with adolescents: the first is that as a period of profound transition, adolescence inevitably throws up relationship and family problems that may not have been previously resolved; the second is that these problems as mentioned throughout the book represent the opportunity for exploration and understanding.

In many cases, understanding how the young person's problem is embedded in the parental interaction can in itself produce dynamic and positive change for the first time in the life of the family as well as the adolescent. This takes into account the re-working of the alliances and attachment within the family. For example, a 17-year-old boy with hitherto compliant behaviour had become involved in school refusal and destructive behaviour. It emerged that he was struggling to avoid a 'blueprint' future mapped out for him by his controlling father. His mother, who had always maintained a passive position in the family, rose up for the first time to assert her authority to challenge the 'blueprint' which helped to free her son from the need to act out in an unhelpful manner. In this example, perceiving the symptom as the opportunity, and not becoming sidelined by the perceived need to get the boy back on track in relation to his schoolwork, enabled us to open up the potential for change that lay dormant within the mother, who could then act in the best interests of her son.

The involvement of parents and caregivers in the therapeutic process

The cornerstone of reconfiguring the psychodynamic approach for time-limited psychotherapy for children and young people is one that does not privilege individual therapy for children and young people in isolation from therapeutic work with parents and caregivers. The reason for this is that it is not solely the psychotherapist's insight that will help the child. Rather, it is the therapist's ability to communicate with the parents in a way that will facilitate *the parents' insight*, which in turn will promote their understanding of the problem and their relationship with the child. Working with parents and caregivers through an interactive approach in which all parties are given voice, is therefore intrinsic to a time-limited approach of psychodynamic therapy with children and young people. It bears no relation to some traditional forms of child psychotherapy in which the child or young person's therapy takes precedence, and in which parents are offered 'parent guidance' or seen once a term to give them feedback about their child's progress with the psychotherapy. At the same time this model is not family therapy, and the focus is primarily on the child and their parents and caregivers, and tends not to involve other family members.

Two core elements become united when we include parents directly in the therapeutic process, which is that we widen the field of inquiry to explore how precisely the child and young person 'speaks the family'. Paradoxically, by widening the field of inquiry in this way, the potential for understanding the problem and addressing it can be carried out in a relatively short space of time.

The parenting and couple relationship

Long-standing researchers and clinicians Philip and Carolyn Cowan have advocated the importance of a focus on couple/parent relationships for many years. Their extensive research supports the finding that a positive change or shift in the couple co-parenting relationship leads to positive outcomes in the care of children (Cowan and Cowan, 2015). The programme 'Parents as Partners' which has been pioneered in the UK based on the Cowans' research as well as that of Marsha and Kyle Pruett (Cowan *et al.*, 2009) has shown very promising results. This programme takes place over 16 weekly sessions and draws on a conceptual framework that incorporates attachment, systemic as well as behavioural ideas. The course explores intergenerational patterns whilst keeping the child in mind. This involves a 'deepening exploration of their relationships with their children'. The findings from the programme demonstrated that improving the quality of the parents' relationship and their interaction with each other regarding their parenting role, additionally appeared to lower the risk of harm to children, as well as reducing the proportion of emotional and behavioural difficulties within the children of these couples. These important findings point to the acknowledgement that we cannot consider therapeutic work with children and young people without considering therapeutic work with their parents and carers (Harold and Leve, 2012). In that respect the child is truly in the parent and the parent is truly in the child.

Building resources around the child and young person; Involving fathers

Since the child/young person/parent interactive approach is so central to time-limited psychotherapy, it is vital that we commence with the right people. In all therapeutic engagement concerning the child and young person, our main aim is to build up resources around the child and this must include the people who have full legal and moral responsibility for the child and young person. These will usually be the biological parents, but may also include foster parents, and the people who have responsibility for the care of the child and young person in the absence of the parents. The absence of fathers in the therapeutic endeavour is a particular problem that needs to be addressed in the first instance. This is often due at least as much to the decision of the therapist, as it is due to the particular family circumstances. Legions of psychotherapists have willingly accepted the singular presence of the mother as the main carer and arbiter of the world of the child, and in doing so have unwittingly entered into collusion with the status quo. This may be due to the fact that the majority of psychotherapists are women who may feel more comfortable with a member of the same sex, and find all manner of rationalisations to justify why it is too hard to involve the father. However, since both parents represent the main resource for the child and young person, it follows that working solely with only one parent significantly limits this resource.

Research into couple relationships carried out by Philip and Carolyn Cowan (2014) and Christopher Clulow (1997, 2001) remind us of the complexities of couple interactions, which have a profound impact on parenting. We may for example, go along with the mother's insistence that her husband refuses to attend the consultation and only later discover that he was never asked. We need to recognise that couples as parents may have their own specific reasons to want to exclude each other, and we would not want to take their justifications for this at face value. In this respect it is helpful to keep in mind as mentioned from the outset, that our role as therapists is intrinsically connected with that of advocacy for the child and young person. Sharing this with parents and stating what constitutes their and our duty of care in relation to the child and young person can offer much needed clarification and cut through potentially unhelpful rivalry and posturing.

By involving fathers we also free ourselves from colluding with some of the current stereotypes regarding men as fathers. This often includes reference to men as preferring to be entirely action-oriented and not having the capacity to listen to the emotional side of a problem, whether it is their own or that of their child.

By taking an unquestioning attitude to such a rigid demarcation between the sexes of who 'owns' or is responsible for the emotional life in the family, we contribute to misrepresenting the enormous contribution men can make to their fathering role, and this undermines the therapeutic task. We may, if we take the time to do so, discover in working with parents that men are just as sensitive to the needs of their children and in some cases more so than their female partners.

The beginning of the therapy

In time-limited psychotherapy it is particularly important to address these collusions and entanglements from the outset and in so doing we create further opportunities to broaden the field of our inquiry. For example, how the referral is made and by whom already gives us important information about the family dynamic. Women may make the initial contact to seek help for a child or young person whom they may refer to consistently as 'my child'. This already gives us an impression of a father who is absent at least in the mind of the mother. An invitation to both parents to attend for an initial consultation may be met with disbelief that the father would be considered of any relevance, and so within minutes of a telephone call we already have an insight into aspects of how this parenting couple operate. This may in turn lead us to begin to make some hypotheses about the presenting problem, even before we have seen the child or young person.

When the parents arrive for the initial consultation, the mother may regale us with the list of the child's misdemeanours or problems, fixing us with her gaze whilst totally excluding the father. He remains silent and from time to time surreptitiously looks at his watch. This scene perfectly encapsulates how the couple communicate and how this does not extend to any notion of shared parenting. The picture is complete when the therapist turns to the father and asks him for his opinion on the problem whereupon he says, 'I don't know because I'm not there'. This response is expected to be understood as referring to the fact that the father works all day and so is not present when the outbursts of the child for example are said to occur, and therefore he cannot be held responsible. Of course his comments tell us so much more, namely that he and his wife have in a sense 'divided up' the family and work tasks so rigidly that whoever is at work does not need to feel responsible for home and family life and vice versa. We are left with a sense that the children in this tightly stratified family have fallen out of the mind of one parent whilst being tightly interwoven in the mind of the other. For the couple this may represent a perfectly reasonable, even positive solution whilst it may in reality be devastating for the children.

This example demonstrates that through widening the field we recognise that everything that is presented is important and offers relevant data. We could therefore not make progress with solely focusing on the child or young person's presenting problem, without first addressing the communication or lack of it on the part of the parents. Once it is made clear that the father is an essential part of the parenting team, and that therapeutic work can only be enhanced by his presence, we may be surprised at how quickly and how dynamically therapy may progress.

In situations where there is chronic conflict between a mother and her son, the absence of the father in an emotional sense, may go to the heart of the problem. This is another example of why rushing to pathologise the child's behaviour may take us into completely the wrong territory. In one such example, an emotionally absent father who was very preoccupied with his work, was encouraged to 'return' to the family after the mother had been struggling with her young son for some time. The mother was heavily identified with her young son and was for much of the time the only parenting presence in the home. She had become concerned however, about her son's attacking behaviour towards her. If we return to our psychodynamic framework, we can recognise the powerful Oedipal conflicts that were at work in this family and how this led the boy to struggle to create some safe space between himself and his mother. The involvement of the father immediately led to an almost total abatement of the problem. In their final session of mother, father and son, the therapist was left with a moving image of the father holding his son aloft as he walked out of the room; the evident joy in the boy's expression was testament to what he had been craving from his father.

Working with the right people: Divorced and blended families

In a world in which parenting configurations have experienced profound change, the issue of blended families, how they are constituted, and how one might work with the children can be a challenging one within the therapeutic encounter. For this reason, it is important to be clear about who needs to be included to address the parenting task, as well as the therapeutic task. Here the issue of the absent or excluded parent and the legal rights and responsibilities of the key people concerned needs to be carefully addressed. We may find ourselves responding to an urgent request from a step parent concerning a child of their partner, in which they present themselves as being the caring 'mother' or 'father'. Where the actual parent exists, it would be a mistake for us to go headlong into accepting the step parent as the person to include in the assessment. There are other examples in which parents may deliberately wish to exclude the biological parent, and present the current partner as having full responsibility. In these cases, our therapeutic task needs to focus on establishing who the key players are, and who needs to be involved in the best interests of the child or young person. We can make a hypothesis in this respect that the confusion that reigns for us in wondering who to include, will be multiplied many times for the children and young people concerned.

Children and young people are acutely observant and often struggle with their parents' wish to create a new 'big happy family' whilst papering over the cracks and differences (Schmidt Neven, 2010). Children and young people recognise that they are not related to the new people who have suddenly arrived in their lives, but they may feel they have no choice in the matter. The issue of maintaining both the appropriate sense of hierarchy and relatedness may become extremely fraught and it is here that the therapist, by maintaining a duty of care and advocating for the child, can contribute significantly to lessening the confusion through clearly stating who has a right and need to be involved in any therapeutic process, and who has not.

Creating a position of trust

While it is important to offer children a separate opportunity to express their feelings about the parental separation or divorce, clinical experience indicates that the direct engagement of parents where possible in this process, creates the best opportunities for long-term positive outcomes. The reason for this is that the child and young person is struggling both with the actual separation of the parents, as well as having to negotiate the emotional mental reality of loss that can never be recovered. For children, this may take the form of a dread of any kind of separation, and a fear of being at the mercy of a panic that either parent may disappear without notice.

Helping the parents to recognise that while their relationship is over, the parenting task continues, needs to be kept at the forefront of our concerns in supporting children and young people. For children, the very fact of parents being able to come together with the therapist to discuss a problem concerning the child is already enormously therapeutic for the child.

The next chapter will address how the clinical method described so far can be translated into clinical technique in working with children, parents and young people.

Chapter 6

The clinical technique in time-limited psychodynamic psychotherapy with children, young people and parents

Setting up the conceptual frame for the therapeutic process

It will be clear from the previous chapters that focused time-limited psychodynamic psychotherapy is dependent on the creation of a distinctive therapeutic frame. The essential components of the therapeutic frame are as follows:

- Being active in the therapeutic process;
- Creating a defined assessment process;
- Taking a therapeutic history;
- Creating a vocabulary for emotional understanding;
- The place of hypothesis, formulation and feedback;
- Using the dynamic nature of the 'here and now';
- Dissolving the boundaries between the consulting room and the wider network.

Starting out

Time-limited psychodynamic psychotherapy involves the setting up of various parameters concerning time, as well as being clear about the aims and objectives of the therapy from the outset. This entails working towards a positive outcome and behavioural change that encompasses not only the child and young person, but also their parents. Time-limited psychodynamic psychotherapy is therefore viewed as a transformative process. Time-limited psychotherapy is considered to be a legitimate treatment mode in its own right in the vast majority of cases, and is not viewed as the lesser option to long-term therapy, or as a holding device until a vacancy occurs for longer term therapy. The clarity of practitioners about these parameters, how these are conveyed to, and understood by, their respective patients, children, parents and young people, is a critical part of the therapeutic process.

How long is time-limited psychotherapy?

The question of how long time-limited psychotherapy should be, is one that is best responded to as flexibly as possible. It is more appropriate to work towards an agreed goal with children and parents, rather than to become fixed on a formula or specific time frame. The very fact that we agree to work on a nominated problem, whether it is the child's presentation of anxiety, sleeping or behavioural difficulties, gives the therapeutic work an impetus and energy thereby creating a partnership in the service of change. Many time-limited programmes of psychotherapy with adults, for example, work within a framework of 16–20 sessions (Lemma *et al.*, 2011). Psychotherapy that continues up to a year and beyond however, would not strictly speaking be considered time-limited. In Australia, adults as well as children and adolescents are each entitled to ten sessions of psychological therapy in a calendar year, for which they receive a financial rebate from the government Medicare system. This means that both parents can attend for therapy as well as their child. (This is separate from psychiatry for which longer term rebates are available.) For good or ill, there is now a tendency for people to consider that their problems need to be resolved within the ten session time frame. However, even given this limited time frame, it is surprising how much can be achieved.

Taking a different view of time and therapeutic outcome

As we know, the readiness of patients for psychotherapeutic work varies widely and we should not underestimate the impact of helping parents particularly, to become more psychologically minded about their children, if this is the main outcome of the therapy. Additionally, when we acknowledge the centrality of the core developmental task and the dynamic nature of growth and change in children and young people, it follows that we utilise a different framework regarding the meaning of time and how this affects therapeutic outcome. In this respect we work *with* the child's inherent capacity for growth and change, rather than solely *on* a pathological construct of their behaviour. Time-limited psychotherapy further enables us to engage with time (which never stands still) as a positive limit as opposed to maintaining an endless open-ended experience in the hope of providing a permanent 'cure' for the child and young person. Time-limited psychodynamic psychotherapy therefore does not aim for fundamental personality change, but is optimistic about the creation of significant change to overcome serious problems, and to promote greater harmony in parent–child relationships.

Additionally, when we take a more dynamic interactive view of the child and young person's problem, it means that the therapist does not have to do all the work. Children, young people and their parents are able, given some time away from the therapy, to 'fill in the gaps' themselves and to 'practise' their newfound skills and understanding. Following the end of a period of therapy it is not unusual, for example, for patients to return months or even years later for further help, which should always be regarded as a sign of success and never as a failure to 'cure'. It demonstrates how these families have benefited from the psychodynamic process and how actively they have utilised it in the service of understanding. They will never return as 'beginners' in the therapeutic process.

In summary, the practitioner from the outset requires a sense of conviction and an appropriate use of authority in setting the parameters for time-limited psychodynamic psychotherapy, both for themselves and for the child, adolescent and parents. Earlier it was stated that the therapist needs to be able to embody the approach in order to be most effective. How this is communicated to parents, children and young people is discussed below.

Being active in the therapeutic process

Time-limited psychotherapy makes a demand on the therapist to be active and communicative at all times. Communication, reflection and observation since they are all of a piece, require to be shared with the parents. In other words, without necessarily jumping to conclusions or offering advice, the therapist shares with parents how they have arrived at making a start in trying to understand the problem. This has two important functions: first, it helps to demystify the therapeutic process and second, it demonstrates how connections can be made between events that at first may appear not to be connected. This function of helping to make these connections is central to the therapeutic process and sets in train an entirely new perspective for many parents about how behaviour can be understood.

Establishing a partnership

The primary focus of being active and communicative with parents is to establish a partnership with them in the service of jointly helping the child and young person. Being able to speak directly and openly to the child and young person is also part of this process. Explaining to children why they have arrived to see the therapist is a critical part of being open and honest with them, and contributes to reducing their anxiety and helping them to engage with the therapeutic process. This is in contrast to a concern that children need to be protected from knowing about themselves and their problems. By being open, direct and communicative, the therapist does not prioritise uncertainty for its own sake or believe that they must wait and not risk making a comment in case it is incorrect. In fact in clinical practice one may at times hear from parents (and children) who have had previous contact with traditional child psychotherapeutic work, that they found it vague and unfocused and received little feedback about what was happening to their child. Part of being active and communicative from the outset involves explaining the time frame to the parents and to the child and young person. Within the time frame the question of who is seen, how often, and when, should be approached flexibly. However, the work with parents remains a constant, and there needs to be agreement about what will be addressed and what will be required from them in terms of their commitment to the process. Clarity in this respect is critical. For example, a practitioner may express disappointment that a father ceases to attend after the first session, but may never in fact have made it clear what their expectations were with respect to his attendance.

Where and when does therapy begin?

The therapeutic process commences with the very first contact with whoever makes the referral. For this reason it is advisable that practitioners make contact by phone themselves with the people they will be seeing, before an appointment time is offered. This means for example, in some practices that the therapist does not accept referrals made via a receptionist as a first cab off the rank approach, as this has the potential to undermine the therapeutic endeavour. The same applies to accepting a referral from a referral team where no consultation has been made with the therapist. Both situations will leave the clinician having to do 'triage' work in the first session, when it may become clear that the client or their problem is not suitable for therapeutic treatment, or their problem does not match the skills of the service. Issues of safety and risk for everyone concerned also need to be taken into account.

The first telephone call with the prospective patient, usually a parent, produces a wealth of information that is not to be underestimated, and the time given to this initial phone call should never be begrudged or rushed. The tone of voice and the way the problem and request for help is presented provides important data. We would always ask the parent to tell us a little about the problem and what they particularly want help with. This need only take a few minutes, but already gives us a picture of what may be happening in the family and enables us to begin to formulate a tentative initial hypothesis.

The initial contact via the telephone call also enables the practitioner to explain how the therapy will be conducted and in this sense asserts the therapeutic frame from the outset. Explaining that both parents (where available) will be required to attend the consultation, as well as ongoing treatment, can result in a response that takes the therapist straight into the heart of the dilemma. For example, a mother who was referring her child broke down and wept on the phone, saying that her husband always made himself unavailable for family commitments. The therapist, by being sympathetic but firm about the father's need to be present was already acting as an ally to the mother, helping her in turn to be firm with her husband, which resulted in his attendance.

Establishing a defined assessment process

The first session: Taking a therapeutic history of the child and the parents

The therapeutic frame involved in time-limited psychodynamic psychotherapy requires a defined assessment process which takes place over two sessions. The first session needs to be devoted solely to seeing the parents to ascertain how they describe the problem, how they have addressed it to date, and what sort of help they are looking for. The first session also offers the setting in which to take the *therapeutic history* both of the child and the parents, which will be described in more detail below.

The first session has three parts: the first being the identification of the problem; what brings the parents to seek help and how they have dealt with the problem so far if at all; the second is the taking of the therapeutic history of the child from birth and the third is taking a therapeutic history of the parents.

Identification of the problem

One of the many reasons it is important to see both parents together wherever possible, is that we may find that they have diametrically opposite views of the problem, or one parent may not believe that there is a problem at all and expects the therapist to convince them.

The assessment process is one of revelation. As explained earlier, once we view the symptom as the opportunity, it becomes the thread in a much larger story; once this thread is pulled, the larger story is unravelled and many more complex layers are revealed. The taking of a therapeutic history is a vital part of this process. This means that we first ask about the history of the child from conception through pregnancy and birth to the present time. Highly significant information is revealed in history taking, but we need to keep in mind that our task is not information gathering in a static factual sense. For this reason, note taking is ill advised and should not be taken during the session as it interferes with the careful observational and listening process. The therapeutic history requires our full attention as to tone and emphasis, and how it leads parents at times on a diversion in which they may reflect on other aspects of their child's life and behaviour that have never been considered before. The taking of the history in the first instance, takes the heat out of the presenting problem and lessens the sense of urgency with respect to finding an immediate solution. In other words it literally gives us pause for thought.

Another issue of significance in taking a history from parents, is that with the ever increasing emphasis on a 'managerial' approach to parenting (Leach, 2004), there is a tendency for them to present themselves as empty of knowledge waiting for the professional to advise them. A focus on 'wrong' or 'right' ways to parent may lead us away from the therapeutic task which is to help parents 'own what they know' and to trust their judgement through tolerating trial and error. This therapeutic task has its parallel in how parents in turn can begin to understand their baby by recognising that rather than having to fill up the baby as an empty vessel, that they are able through a partnership with the infant to elicit what the baby already knows.

Taking a therapeutic history of the child

The questions asked about the child's history are concerned with exploring with the parents the circumstances of the pregnancy, the experience of the birth and how the child has negotiated the normal milestones of development. These milestones include, feeding, sleeping, toileting and socialising; how the child has managed separations from the parents, such as going to childcare, kindergarten and school; illnesses the child may have had; how the child performs academically; the child's interests and activities. On occasion, parents may come to the first session in a defensive mode denying that there is a problem, because the concerns about their child have been raised elsewhere, such as by the school. Allowing the parents to take the time to respond to the questions about the child's everyday life may bring home to them the realisation that all is not as they have wanted to assume.

Key points to keep in mind: Resisting being 'blinded' by the symptom

We keep in mind that the *presenting problem* of the child and young person represents the entry point to the therapeutic service. We make an assumption that it is not the *real problem* in the sense of containing the total picture. By resisting the urge to become 'blinded by the symptom' we also exercise caution in attributing a label to the presenting problem. In summary, in taking a therapeutic history and hearing about the problem, we recognise the following:

*   What you see is rarely what you get;
*   We are concerned with the unravelling of meaning not pathology;
*   We ask questions that open up communication rather than closing it down;
*   We understand presenting problems not as existing in a concrete sense *within* the child and young person, but being more likely to be a manifestation of what is taking place *between* the child, the young person and their parents and the broader family;
*   The presenting problem may therefore be perceived as personifying the struggle of the child or young person to make sense of their experience.

Taking a therapeutic history of the parents

Similarly to taking the child's history, taking a history of the parents' lives and childhood experiences, has a particular power as it goes beyond the bare assembling of facts and offers parents the opportunity to hear themselves perhaps for the first time discuss issues that may never previously have been discussed, or were overlooked. The simple request to hear the parents' story of their lives as children growing up, can be made by saying that the way we were parented, influences the way we parent our children. This simple statement offers parents respite from the pressing problem of what to do about their child's problem. It also immediately opens up the communication and moves from one that starts off as linear and individually centred, to one that becomes interactive, multi-faceted and inter-generational. For example, where a child presents with particular social and communication problems, a question about whether anyone else in either family may have had a similar problem, will probably initially elicit a negative response whereas the exploration of the history as it unfolds, may reveal a description of a brother or sister who had very similar problems.

The therapeutic history and the rule of three

The presence of the therapist as the third party is often significant in giving permission to one or other of the parents to communicate things that may have hitherto been denied or kept secret. Taking a history of the parents takes them back into their childhoods where painful events have been experienced that remain unresolved. The tone and manner of communication provides insight into how these experiences have been lived with, and in many cases not metabolised. For example, a parent may describe a traumatic childhood filled with loss and bereavement as 'normal' and the flat tone of their voice suggests the enormity of these experiences that they were not able to make sense of, as they were barely acknowledged by their own parents, or important people in their lives.

How this experience and the way it is communicated can be connected with the presenting problem is often illuminating. For example, the presentation of high levels of anxiety about separation in the child may be the most visible manifestation of a long-standing but denied anxiety in the parent. Where both parents are present, this has the advantage of providing the counterpoint between one parent's history and the other. One parent may perceive their own history as troubled and volatile, and their partner's as happy and somewhat idealised. Closer examination through the recounting of the family history may reveal a very different picture in which for example, the idealised family may have maintained itself through denying painful events. Some parents may demonstrate a kind of amnesia about their childhoods and growing up, which may lead the other partner to try to help them fill the gaps.

The most significant function of the telling of the parental history is that by doing so, it inevitably contributes to the commencement of the therapeutic process. The reason for this is that when the presentation of the child or young person's problem is followed by the taking of a history of the parents, this creates opportunities for important connections to begin to be made that underpin the task of therapy. By so doing, it also encourages a space for reflection, which further contributes to the therapeutic process.

History taking with single, divorced and bereaved parents

The need for history taking is no less critical for parents who are parenting on their own, or working out a parenting arrangement through divorce and separation. In the latter it is ideal if both parents can be facilitated to attend if this is a possibility. Whilst a referral may be made by either parent father or mother, it is important that the therapist communicates with each party separately in order to introduce themselves and set up joint appointments, and not make either parent the message taker. This enables the therapist to maintain a position of transparency and even-handedness, that is in the best interests of the child. As we know, children can produce problems which force their parents to come together. In one such example, a mother contacted the therapist to complain about the impact on her daughter of what she considered to be inappropriate social contacts of the father in the course of an access visit. The involvement of the father revealed that the complaint had been taken out of context and was somewhat exaggerated. However most importantly, it revealed a high level of separation anxiety in the daughter connected with both parents that had hitherto been glossed over, but actually needed urgent attention. In this context the coming together of the parents in the service of trying to help their daughter, was in itself therapeutic for the child.

There are instances of course in which it is not possible to see both parents for reasons connected with potential emotional or physical violence, where consideration of the safety of the patient (and the therapist) is paramount. In these situations the taking of a history is even more critical in that it throws light on how people have found their way into destructive relationships and how this influences their fear of the future for their children.

Summarising the problem: Towards articulating a formulation

The importance of the therapist to be active and communicative has been emphasised throughout, and comes to the fore at the end of each of the assessment sessions. At the end of the first session in which parents have described the problem, their attempts at dealing with it, the history of their child and their own history, we are in a position to begin to work towards a formulation. Creating points of connection is critical in time-limited therapy. At the end of the first session it is the task of the therapist to draw together what they have heard thus far and begin to make possible links.

The requirement here is not to make a perfect or totally accurate formulation, but to show the parents that the therapist has listened carefully to what has been said and that the behaviour of the child or young person may be understood as, for example, being a response to a loss, or difficult early history, or even a manifestation of confusion, if the parents have very different views on how to parent.

A further demand of a psychotherapist with experience and training in work with children and young people is to be able to identify the possibility that the presenting problem indicates a disturbance that is intrinsic to the child, such as being on the autism spectrum, or having a developmental problem, including cognitive deficits. It is vital in this regard to ensure that a referral is made to other appropriate professionals.

Chapter 7

Placing the child and young person in the therapeutic frame

Preparing the child and young person for the assessment process

At the end of the first session and meeting with the parents or parent, the scene is set to invite the child or young person into the assessment process. Time needs to be given to advise the parents on how to prepare their child and what to say. Parents are encouraged to be completely truthful about the problem and their concerns, and to be truthful about who the therapist is and what their focus will be. How parents listen to this preparation or not, and what they make of it when they inform their child of the appointment, provides helpful data about how the family communicates. For young children it is advised that parents do not tell their child that they are going to see 'a lady with toys' or 'a friend' as even young children demonstrate an immediate grasp of what is at stake. In some cases, the complete lack of preparation of the child, or merely informing them in the car on the way to the session, gives us important information about the parents' ambivalence and also reflects a level of unconscious aggression towards the child, which needs to be noted. We may speculate for example, that a parent who has survived a cruel and uncaring childhood may feel impelled to repeat something similar with their own child, in not preparing them properly for the session.

Part two of the assessment: Meeting with the child, young person and parents

The second session which comprises the meeting with the child or young person and their parents, is intended to give the child or young person an opportunity to speak about the problem initially with their parents present, and then to spend time with the psychotherapist on their own to give their view of the problem, or any other issue they may wish to raise. The task of the psychotherapist is to find ways of integrating these two sets of information, and to communicate these at the end of the session to both the parents, and the child or young person, in a manner that opens up a meaningful dialogue. The final part of the session brings parents and child/young person together to reflect on the problem and how it may be approached, followed by a plan and agreement for ongoing therapy.

The beginning of this second assessment session with the child/young person and their parents or parent is crucial in identifying how the child or young person has been prepared for the consultation. It also provides an opportunity for the child or young person to hear about the concerns of the parents and to offer their own version of events. For young children whose parents may complain about their impulsive or aggressive behaviour, it is important to let the child know that they are not in any trouble, whilst simultaneously maintaining the boundaries of the consulting room and the boundaries of the assessment process. This would involve for example, not allowing a young child to run out of the room, try to damage the furniture or imperiously demand that their parents take them home, and try to punish their parents by hitting or kicking them if they decline. When the therapist is active and protective, and asserts the rules of the consulting room in a kind but firm manner which does not allow the child to dictate to the adults, it contains the child's omnipotence and already begins to model to the parents a different way of coping with the problem.

Encouraging communication

Talking with young children directly and openly about why they are seeing the therapist also indicates to parents that emotional matters can be talked about reflectively, rather than simply be reacted to. When young children come into a room with their parents in which there are toys, they are instinctively drawn to play with the toys, while their parents are left to talk with the therapist. However, by insisting that the child is part of the conversation from the outset however briefly, this sets the scene for a new way of communicating, talking and listening (Schmidt Neven, 2002).

For the second part of the second session, the child is alone with the therapist. Young children generally will avail themselves of the toys, drawing materials and doll's house with a small doll family and furniture. It is of interest to the therapist to pay attention to the particular toys that the child enjoys playing with, their capacity for a fantasy life and imaginative play, or their inclination to be quickly bored. The connection with the parent in the waiting room is always present, sometimes in the form of anxiety when the child asks to see their parents if the separation cannot be tolerated. At times, children want to create something they can show their parents. Problematic relationships with either or both parents may be demonstrated through for example, the drawing of excessive love hearts which are then folded up and offered as a gift for the returning parent.

There are many examples of children who are enormously relieved to have the opportunity to speak to the therapist directly, and have so much to say about their predicament, that they ignore the toys and go straight into the conversation with the therapist to explain what is happening to them. For example, a boy of eight caught up in the aftermath of his parents' acrimonious divorce, felt the enormous burden of the problem, and struggled to take an even-handed approach towards them. He described a situation all too typical of needing to switch off from hearing his father speak about his mother in an abusive manner. He informed the therapist that he could not allow his disappointment with his father to override his love for his father, but he feared that this might happen.

It has been stated earlier that we should be cautious about prematurely de-coupling adolescents and young people from their parents in an attempt to offer them an experience of independence. We may hypothesise that the problems adolescents bring are still so encapsulated within the family dynamic, so that wherever possible, attempts should be made to help the adolescent within the family context. Suicidal ideation, cutting, and other self-destructive impulses can be seen to represent an impasse for the young person, who feels that they have no other means of communication primarily with their parents. The causes may be complex, but maintaining the linkages with parents holds out hope that they, and their parents, can be helped to begin the process of opening up communication.

Considerations of technique: Looking for capacity

In the part of the assessment session that is devoted to time alone with the child and young person, our focus is on looking for, and assessing what may be described as *capacity* in the child and young person. Capacity refers to the ability of the child or young person to communicate through words or play, something of their experience, and the ability in even a small way to be able to step back and think about their actions. Looking out for capacity is particularly important when a child or young person is described in pejorative terms, or where the parents' own problems have become projected onto the child. Parents' assumption of the helplessness and hopelessness of the child or young person may also be completely at odds with what they are actually capable of. For example, an adolescent boy with severe anxiety and obsessive behaviours displayed a surprising sense of humour and lightness of touch with respect to describing his favourite activities. This did not detract from the seriousness of the problem, but gave the therapist important insight into his potential capacity for therapeutic work. This recognition enabled the therapist in turn to support his parents to heighten the bar with respect to their expectations of him.

Feedback and forward planning

Since the second session has offered an opportunity for the child/young person and their parents to talk together, as well as for the child/young person to talk separately, the psychotherapist now goes one step further in elaborating a formulation about the problem to both parties. This first, takes the form of giving the parents some brief feedback about the meeting with the child. This does not entail a detailed account of everything that was said, but is intended to share with the parents the therapist's impression of the child, and how they used the therapeutic encounter. For example, by relating to the parents of the adolescent boy described above, that their son had a delightful sense of humour, and how despite the seriousness of the problem, this indicated his wish to be different and more light-hearted, this eased their panic and anxiety. Children who have been described by their parents as aggressive, may show a very different side of themselves to the therapist, and may through their play or communication, indicate how their aggression covers underlying fear and anxiety. This is a critical piece of information that would need to be shared with parents, which brings us back to the essential linking and meaning-making task of the therapeutic process.

The final part of this second session brings everyone together, the parents and the child or young person. The therapist presents a brief summary of what has been observed, and what sense the therapist has made of what has been communicated. Whilst this summarising and confirming takes place at some level throughout the assessment, the coming together of the child, young person and their parents at the end of the session, allows this to be re-addressed. It also takes into account any differing views that may be expressed at this point. Negotiating a treatment plan arises directly from this formulation, and requires the agreement of all concerned. Even young children when they recognise that they are listened to, and taken seriously, can be part of this process.

A living cooperative endeavour

As such, the treatment plan becomes a living cooperative endeavour rather than one that seeks the disposal of the problem within the child. The treatment plan whilst acknowledging the inevitable interactive nature of the problem, needs to make room for the child/young person and their parents, to have the space to consider these issues separately as well as together. For this reason, the initial assessment is followed by continuing separate sessions for the child or young person, as well as separate sessions for the parents. Joint sessions with the parents and child/young person are organised at various points in the course of the treatment, as particular issues come to light, or where greater clarification is required. This is particularly useful where for example, parents complain about the challenging and aggressive behaviour of their child but feel at a loss with respect to how to handle this. The initial assessment may reveal that there is a degree of uncertainty and anxiety in the child, that underlies their aggression, whilst the parents are confused about the need to set appropriate limits and boundaries. The separate sessions then enable the child to give voice to their worries, and for the parents to begin to understand how to assume their authority. Once this has been explored, a joint meeting with the support of the therapist can provide a rewarding experience in which the parents can clarify their requests to the child, and explain the ground rules of the household. This in turn promotes a greater sense of containment for the child, and of knowing literally where he or she stands.

Continuing the treatment

Given that at least one parent will be present at the individual sessions with the child or young person, unless they can travel on their own, there are likely to be inevitable outbursts or breakdowns in communication preceding the session, that 'speak' the core problem with which we are concerned. Here it is important to view this, similarly to the symptom, as *the opportunity* and a source of discovery that represents rich data about what is actually taking place between the child/young person and their parents. As people feel more relaxed and trusting towards the therapist, they will be more inclined to bring the truth of their experiences and feelings, and this will not be presented in a tidy manner. In these situations, the dynamic of the 'here and now' discussed in more detail below, comes particularly to the fore. It can therefore be of great benefit to spend time both with the child and parent at the start and end of each session to clarify what has taken place.

We build on the assumption that long-standing dysfunctional behaviours between parents and child will be bound to be repeated in the therapeutic encounter. For example, parents may want their child to take a more independent stance about their problems, but they may get cold feet when this creates some discomfort in the child. They may also have misgivings about the therapy when their child goes from being enthusiastic about the sessions, to wanting their parents to inform the therapist that they no longer wish to attend. Hence, we may need to tease out where the resistance lies, and whether the child may actually be a mouthpiece for the parents.

It is for these reasons that the involvement of parents in the therapeutic process is essential. This is predicated on the assumption that children cannot make changes to their lives, if there is no receptive container in which these changes can be lived out. Since parents hopefully act psychologically as containers for their children, then in turn, the therapist must provide containment for parents so that they can embark on making the appropriate changes.

Looking for leverage

As we know from professional experience, things do not always go according to plan. Despite our best efforts, one parent may drop out of therapy, or the child or young person may be so resistant to therapy that it is not possible to continue with them. Where do we go from here? As mentioned above, in the vast majority of cases these issues will reflect the family and parent/child dynamic that has been present for a number of years. The investment of both parents and children is very high in not having this dynamic disturbed, certainly not by the therapist. In this situation we return to our consideration of what has been described as *capacity*; in other words, who amongst the people who have presented themselves to the therapist has the capacity and will to continue with the therapeutic process? (See de Shazer, 1988).

Taking a systemic view enables us to look for leverage in order to create change. We know from family therapy and systemic theory that change in one part of a system will inevitably lead to change in another part. The heavily resistant father, or mother, or child, or young person has an omnipotent belief that their refusal to continue with the therapy will mean that everyone will give up, and follow them back into the dysfunctional status quo. Or we may come across a system in which everyone is waiting for someone else to change, before they feel that anything can be done; the wife waits for her husband to change and both may be waiting for their child to change.

By assessing capacity and looking for leverage, we may for the first time in these predicaments be in a position to help challenge these assumptions and positions, and begin to lay the groundwork for health and growth. For example, a mother by insisting on her right to continue in the therapy gives a strong message to her resistant husband that she is a separate person, and as such of course she has separate legal responsibilities towards the children. A controlling adolescent who walks out of the therapy may be surprised to find that his parents do not follow him, and he has to accept that he has opted out of the opportunity to present his point of view in the continuing discussions. Even children with disorders such as an autism spectrum disorder, can therapeutically benefit from a challenge to the status quo in which their anxiety and rigidity completely engulfs the family. When given sufficient therapeutic support, parents can make changes and set limits and boundaries that can make life more liveable not only for the family as a whole, but may succeed in reducing the anxiety and rigidity in the child.

In summary the assessment process and follow up involves attention to the Five Cs:

* **Coherence** – Giving behaviour meaning – Allowing parents and children and young people to hear themselves;
* **Continuity** – Understanding how the past affects the present; the impact of intergenerational experience;
* **Context** – Putting the problem into a family meaning making context;
* **Containment** – The professional making it possible to reflect on and understand the experience and the problem;
* **Consistency** – The professional maintaining the therapeutic frame for this exploration to occur.

Dissolving the boundaries between the therapist and the wider network

Looking for leverage and capacity naturally leads us to consider the next step in time-limited psychotherapy with children, parents and young people. This is that at times, the therapeutic endeavour needs to include additionally, the broader network that surrounds the child. We acknowledge that children and young people are connected with schools, kindergartens, childcare centres, and in some cases with other professional services. The degree, to which professional help can be provided to these services as additional support, is often critical to working towards a positive outcome. For example, how do we approach a situation where children and young people are referred for long-standing problems associated with chronic pain for which no organic cause can be found despite extensive investigations? The complexity of this problem is well known to hospital outpatient services in particular, and also to child psychotherapists. Walker (2015) describes working with these children and young people as requiring a flexible approach that is also centred on helping the family to 'understand' the symptom and deal with the anxieties that arise from it. The following example illustrates how this may be achieved.

An adolescent in transition

A 14-year-old girl was referred for psychotherapy by her parents, following a long period of investigation for pain in her limbs, for which no organic cause could be found. It was clear from the outset that she was very resistant to any therapeutic work and her responses were limited and defensive, which indicated her anxiety about having her symptoms challenged, as these had had some protective function for her in the face of long-standing family difficulties. She had moved from another town where she had been barely able to attend the local school because of her condition and had had many absent days. At the point at which her condition had begun to improve slightly, her parents were determined to enrol her in a new school so that she could make 'a fresh start'. The therapist was concerned given her long absence from the routine of school, that full time attendance in this new school environment might prove a huge obstacle for her. Rather than making a 'fresh start', she would most likely relapse, and return to her old position of incapacity in the family. The therapist therefore recommended that she not attend for a full day at least for the first term, but only for a three-hour morning session. This variation on the paradoxical injunction was an attempt to anticipate that if she attended for a full day of school, the strain would bring on a collapse and lead to a justification not to continue at school. The therapist also believed that given the entrenched and long-standing nature of the problem, that it would require active involvement on the part of the school and their agreement that she only attend for three hours to start with.

   With the consent of the parents, the therapist visited the school where she found the key staff members hugely relieved that they could be participants in the treatment plan as they were uncertain how to proceed. They said that they were so often overlooked and welcomed the opportunity to liaise with the therapist as well as with the parents. In this example, we can see how attention to *capacity* and *looking for leverage* within the school system, combined to provide a critical safety net for the young girl. This resulted in a successful transition for her, and a sense of achievement over time, when she increased the hours of her attendance and became involved in school life.

One may find many other examples of how by dissolving the boundaries between the therapist and the wider network, we make things more workable and liveable for children and young people. Connecting with childcare centres and kindergartens has the benefit of casting our assessment and diagnostic web much wider in the service of understanding children's behaviour. This is particularly relevant in relation to trying to understand how it is that the developmental process can become impeded.

Time-limited psychotherapy with children and young people experiencing loss and trauma

Therapeutic work with children and young people who have experienced significant abuse, loss and trauma, poses a major challenge for all who are involved in their care. The challenges involved in trying to help these often very damaged children and young people, tend to evoke in professionals, an inclination towards either despair or omnipotence. In the case of the latter, it would be wise to carefully 'read the labels' of therapies and programmes that present their snappy euphemistic titles, claiming to be 'evidence-based' and promise to undo a lifetime of misery and trauma in a stroke (Schmidt Neven, 2010). We would also want to avoid the pitfalls of either trying to get rid of troublesome behaviour through cognitive behavioural therapy, or maintain a belief that only long-term psychotherapy will make any difference.

In this respect we have to keep in mind that many deprived and deeply troubled children and young people, do not easily fit into one to one therapy, nor do they necessarily find it beneficial. This is due at least in part to their profoundly disordered relationships that have been characterised by abuse and neglect. In this context, time-limited psychotherapy has a helpful role to play in two key areas: given the very nature of a time-limited approach, this may be perceived as less threatening by the child and young person; second, there is the emphasis on working with children and young people in the *total field*. The fact that therapeutic contact can be time-limited may give children and young people a sense of control where this has largely been removed from them. Moreover, it holds out the promise that the child and young person can always return later to continue the therapy or focus on a particular area. The incorporation of the *total field* is crucial in therapeutic work with children and young people whose very connections with family and the community may hang on a thread through disruptive and destructive experiences. Here, the focus on dissolving the boundaries between the clinical setting and the broader network, comes into its own and provides a much needed protective safety net. The technique of finding the leverage is also at work in this process, where the child and young person may find a helpful connection with another professional, such as a teacher, social worker, or community worker. In this context, there is a parallel process in finding capacity in the referred child and young person and finding capacity in the system that surrounds them. Taking an inclusive rather than an exclusive approach means that we include foster parents and others who act in a parenting capacity as part of the *total field*.

The place of hypothesis formulation and feedback

It will have become clear by now that this framework of time-limited psychodynamic psychotherapy is one that is continuously active and reflective, and takes a direct, transparent and interactive approach to working with children, parents and young people. Within this model, the creation of hypothesis and formulation represent the engine room of the approach. How the clinicians particularly those in training, can be helped to develop a systematic approach to the formulation of clinical problems is described in detail in an excellent paper by Havighurst and Downey (2009). The psychologist authors pose the question of how are we to make sense of the stories told to us by the families we see, given our contemporary understanding of the literature and clinical evidence concerning development, relationships and personality functioning? The authors advocate an approach that is not simply 'a description of symptoms' but one that identifies 'patterns of difficulties and strengths through a rich understanding of the case history and current dynamics' (Havighurst and Downey, 2009, p.252).

The authors propose a bio-psycho-social model of working towards a formulation that encompasses predisposing, precipitating, perpetuating and protective factors. They describe how each of these steps can be broken down, and how data can be systematically collected in order to arrive at a meaningful formulation known as *the mindful formulation*. Arriving at the formulation enables the practitioner in turn to make appropriate recommendations for treatment. It is interesting to note that *the mindful formulation* does not advocate any particular therapeutic orientation, but emphasises instead, the need to create a discrete period of assessment that should not get lost within a contemporary cost-cutting climate. Most significantly, the paper highlights the need for clinicians to move away from a narrow problem-based focus of blaming either the child or the parent, to one that explores individual child and parent intra- and inter-personal dynamics, as well as systemic and intergenerational factors all of which throw light on the presenting problem.

Havighurst and Downey emphasise the importance of involving fathers in this process, who as they point out, have become marginalised from many therapeutic services. The inclusion of fathers also leads to another key element in the formulation process, which at its best is a collaborative exercise. This includes the opinion and hypotheses of the clients or patients themselves. Working with parents in partnership, and providing containment for them, is intrinsic to this collaborative process. This takes place through a review and reframing of the problem as the therapy progresses, which comes particularly to the fore in time-limited psychodynamic psychotherapy through working with what takes place in the 'here and now'.

The dynamic nature of the 'here and now'

A particular feature of time-limited psychodynamic psychotherapy is how, because of the time limitation, as well as the opportunity for individual and conjoint work, it introduces a level of intensity into the clinical interchange which brings to the fore many of Luborsky's 'core conflictual' elements of the child and family dynamic. These elements would in traditional child psychotherapy tend to take a considerable time to emerge, or may never come to the fore. In time-limited therapy, particularly in conjoint sessions with the child and parents, it is remarkable to observe how in the 'here and now' of the sessions, children demonstrate through their actions, the need to draw the parents' as well as therapist's attention to the dilemmas with which they are faced. Often it is these wordless experiences in the 'here and now' that more than any discussion can illuminate the core unconscious dilemma. It is these 'here and now' experiences coming explicitly to the fore in time-limited psychotherapy, that help move the therapeutic process forward by leaps and bounds.

In one such example, a mother complained about the challenging behaviour of her young child which had arisen mainly because of earlier turmoil in their lives. Her behaviour towards him tended to be inconsistent and when things were at their worst between them she expressed the belief that he hated her. The therapist observed that in fact the child was closely attached to his mother, but was at times uncertain about how to approach her. His struggle with his loving and hateful feelings were dramatically revealed when in one joint session in which his father was also present, the little boy went over to his mother to plant a kiss on her cheek. However, as he did so, he also bared his teeth.

It was an action that perfectly encapsulated Shedler's description of how the psychodynamic approach can illuminate 'inner contradictions'.

The therapist, who saw what had taken place, whilst the mother was not entirely aware of it, was able through gentle humour to explore with both the parents and the child what was being communicated. This in turn opened up a discussion about having mixed feelings both as parents and as children, and how this need not be a frightening or destructive emotional state of mind.

There are many other examples of children who enact the drama of their conflicts in the session for the benefit of their parents, in the hope that the therapist will be able to understand what is being 'said' and to act as facilitator and translator. One example refers to a confusion about hierarchy between parents and children, particularly when parents feel overwhelmed with the task of being in charge and try to flatten out the hierarchy by being the child's 'friend'. How this is manifested in the clinical sessions may vary, and may tend to take the form of the child monopolising the parent, and not allowing them to speak, or denigrating them, or talking to them as though they are a version of themselves. The therapist may also be drawn into this enactment, but by being active and communicative in the 'here and now' can help both the parents and the child to undo some of these entanglements.

What happens to the transference?

In this interactive approach, that encompasses the child, young person and their parents and caregivers, the transference is understood and responded to differently, from that of traditional individual psychotherapy. In the latter, it is the relationship between the patient, child, or adult and the psychotherapist, that is the constant and the primary vehicle through which early experience is enacted and can be reflected upon. In the interactive time-limited approach with children, young people and their parents, whilst the transference with respect to the patient–therapist relationship is noted throughout, it is kept more in mind than immediately commented upon. The reason for this is that we are concerned to enable the parents to become a parenting team, and to promote and restore their relationship with their child. We are therefore primarily encouraging the exploration of the relationships *between* these family members and not specifically with ourselves, as therapists. In this context, transference interpretations are most useful when for some reason the treatment process is not proceeding well, or there is a sudden and apparently unexplained decision on the part of the parents, or the child and young person, to terminate the therapy.

Fluidity and transformation in time-limited psychotherapy

As mentioned earlier, the therapeutic technique in time-limited psychodynamic psychotherapy involves a degree of intensity in working towards a positive outcome. This, together with the fact that we may for the first time have all the key players available, creates an impetus for what may be described as *transformative occurrences* in the therapy. When we recognise the essential fluidity of the child/adolescent/parent interaction, it is often brought home to us how the child or adolescent's presenting problem represents as Winnicott described it, 'a latent displaced expression of parental states'. In other words, we may (without denying the reality of the challenges experienced) view the child's or adolescent's problems as a kind of figment of the parents' imagination. Our job as psychotherapists is not to get bogged down in this presenting symptomatology, but to help bring the real child and adolescent into focus, through perceiving their symptoms as the opportunity. A striking outcome of this process is that the focus of concern almost invariably shifts onto either both the parents, or one individual parent. It is not unusual for this to occur, bringing to the fore long-standing conflicts, unresolved mourning, trauma and unhappiness that reside in one or both parents.

The journey from children to parents and back

This process paradoxically presents us with the opportunity to begin to work with the 'right' person. In one such example, parents brought their nearly four-year-old son to the therapist because of their concerns about his reluctance to toilet train. It emerged that the parents had a very busy work schedule and had set up routines in their home in almost militaristic style. This suggested an anxiety that chaos would reign if these schedules were not adhered to. The toileting problem ceased almost immediately once the parents relaxed their rigid stance and the child was happy to be included directly in discussions about his 'ownership' of his body. However, some other more minor symptoms persisted and the mother particularly reported similar concerns with her other children, and was critical of them when they were not as careful or tidy as she wanted them to be. It became clear to the therapist that the need for control resided principally in the mother, and it was suggested that they meet separately to discuss this further. Given that there had already been a positive outcome for her child, the mother was prepared to cooperate with this suggestion. Through these sessions, a picture emerged of the mother growing up as a child and adolescent, having to manage high levels of parental dysfunction. Her need for order and rigidity was an appropriate response to the disorder and chaos she had experienced in her earlier life. This important insight created a transformative experience for the mother with respect to lessening her demands on herself, and becoming more emotionally available to her children.

There are other examples where parents may present with high levels of conflict about how they parent together, and are critical of each other. On occasion, the conflict may be so high that the parents cannot agree to bring their child to therapy even though they acknowledge that there is a problem. One may hypothesise that they may be reluctant to find a solution to the child's problem, since the child's difficulties have an underlying function in maintaining their relationship. Making the suggestion to shift the focus entirely away from the child is then helpful. This may involve continued work with the parenting couple or with one of the parents. The important task is to gain clarity about where the problem actually lies.

In summary, therapeutic work with children, young people and their parents because it is intrinsically dynamic, and encompasses the four domains of the intra-psychic, the inter-personal, the systemic and the environmental, represents a journey in which there is rarely a path that leads directly from A to B. As psychotherapists therefore, we need to be prepared to be agile and open to the change of direction. In so doing, we promote the best interests of children and young people, as well as the capacity of their parents to care for them.

Chapter 8

Clinical challenges

The potential of the time-limited model

Clinical challenges

The previous three chapters have described the essential method and technique of time-limited psychodynamic psychotherapy and how the child and young person can be placed within this therapeutic frame. This chapter will focus on how this model can be applied with respect to some of the clinical challenges that are presented to clinicians who work with children, young people and their parents. Clinicians who have worked for many years in the field may identify two particular areas that pose challenges in the therapeutic encounter. The first is that of emotional and psychological problems that present as embedded within the child and young person. These generally take the form of obsessive behaviours. They may also take the form of physical problems for which no organic cause can be found. The second area of concern for many clinicians is that of the often apparent confusion on the part of parents about their parenting task and responsibilities. These confusions in turn give rise to fraught child/adolescent/parent interaction in which the challenging behaviour of the child becomes the focus of attention. The fundamental assumption made here is that these problems in almost all cases will not be responsive to the taking of a solely individually focused therapeutic approach. They have to be interpreted more broadly to take into account the links between the intra-psychic, the interpersonal, the social and the systemic domains, and these need to be reflected in the therapeutic work. The following account of responding to these clinical challenges in the context of time-limited therapy is intended to offer an aide to practice through considering this more interactive approach.

Revisiting the use of formulation

As experienced clinicians we come to challenging problems with assumptions about why they are presented at a particular point in time, and how societal changes may affect both the presentation of the problems, and the way in which parents and indeed professionals try to make sense of them. As discussed throughout the book this means that we start from the position of creating the widest context for understanding, and do not foreclose on narrow circumscribed definitions of the problem. This brings us back to the question of formulation and how the attention given to the formulation process is essential to the successful practice of time-limited therapy. The Division of Clinical Psychology of the British Psychological Society (2011) in their Guidelines on the use of psychological formulation, emphasise throughout how formulation has personal meaning at its core. This personal meaning is always located within a systemic, organisational and societal context. Whilst the Guidelines describe recommended practice for clinical psychologists, they are equally applicable to all professionals working in the mental health field. As pointed out in the Guidelines, a psychological formulation is concerned with attending to the summarising and integrating of the knowledge and information that has been acquired in the assessment process. As in psychotherapy, the formulation process prioritises the use of reflective practice. Most importantly the Guidelines consider that formulation represents 'a shared narrative' that is constructed together with the people we are trying to help. Ultimately, a formulation is not a final statement or a tablet of stone. As such, it allows for new information and understanding to be included as this becomes available. This new information may contradict or amplify what has gone before. Thus the process of formulation, which takes place over a number of steps, may be perceived as a series of hypotheses that are constructed, tested and if required, modified through reflection on clinical experience. The Division of Psychology Guidelines highlight a critical element in the construction of the formulation process, by asserting that best practice in clinical formulation is 'person-specific not problem-specific'. This immediately opens up a more dynamic and relationship centred form of clinical practice that goes beyond the constraints of the bio-medical models described earlier.

Applying the practice framework to clinical challenges

How can we apply understanding of the uses of formulation, as well as the essential components presented of the practice of time-limited psychotherapy to embedded emotional problems within the child and young person? Additionally, how can we apply these principles in therapeutic practice with parents regarding apparent confusions about parenting tasks and responsibilities? In what follows there is first a description of how this model of time-limited psychotherapy can be applied in working with adolescents who present with what may be identified as an embedded problem, such as obsessive beliefs and behaviour. This is then followed by a description of ways the time-limited model can be employed in working with younger children with physical problems for which no organic cause can be found. Finally, in the following chapter the time-limited practice framework will be discussed in relation to therapeutic work with parents.

Embedded problems within the adolescent

Obsessive beliefs and behaviour tend to form around particular convictions about a truth concerning the self, others or certain aspects of the immediate environment. These 'truths' have very little or no connection with actual reality. Often they appear as the distinct opposite of what is actually taking place. Once the conviction becomes embedded, this then tends to give rise to behaviours and statements that are tasked with the need to preserve and reinforce the original conviction. As these behaviours and statements continue to take precedence, they inevitably have an impact on the day-to-day life of the adolescent with respect to increasing anxiety to high levels, limiting enjoyment, friendships and relaxation. A psychodynamic perspective would take the view that the very intensity with which the obsessive belief is pursued provides important information, as this suggests that the belief covers, or is a diversion from, other deeper concerns or worries that cannot be expressed. These deeper concerns and worries would tend to be concerned with anxieties about the self, with identity and with close personal and family relationships. The obsessive behaviour may thus be viewed as a kind of temporary staging post for thoughts, wishes and fears that are too dangerous to be articulated through normal channels.

Why parents need to be involved

As discussed earlier, this model of time-limited psychotherapy does not de-couple adolescents and young people from their parents when it comes to addressing their psychological and emotional problems. In fact it takes a strong relationship-based approach to the embedded problem in the adolescent and young person, perceiving it at all times as a communication to the parents, however confused and disturbing it may be. This integral therapeutic model therefore involves working both with the young person and their parents separately and jointly to address the difficulty. Because the embedded problem is viewed as intrinsic to the family dynamic and family system, by separating it out and working solely with the young person, this inevitably leads to a problem-centred rather than a person-in-relation centred focus. The problem-centred focus in turn is more likely to favour a bio-medical construction, which sets the young person onto the path of the mental health patient trajectory with a potentially poor outcome. In contrast to this, the rationale is that since the young person and their parents and family are often trapped in the problem together, any therapeutic work should attend to widening the frame. This must involve parents, but it may also involve the school and other professionals and services that have an important link with, and influence on, the young person.

The assessment and formulation process with parents

Examples of embedded problems

Examples of embedded problems in the adolescent and young person may take a number of different forms. For example, they may have a fear that despite being academically competent or even gifted, that they will fail at school and in life unless they work all hours. Some obsessive behaviours may take the form of the young person being preoccupied with a part of their body, usually their face, nose or hairline. Often these behaviours and fears are accompanied by particular rituals in which the young person tries to involve their parents and becomes furious if they refuse.

When parents first arrive to meet the therapist to discuss the embedded problem of their son or daughter, we can assume that they have inevitably become caught up and encapsulated in the problem themselves. It is understandable that their first request is to focus on the problem as though it stands alone or can be separately identified and therefore separately treated. By taking a meaning making stance and one that considers a broader formulation, we already introduce a different dimension into the therapeutic process. We understand that the rigidity and insistence of the young person about their perspective of themselves and the problem, has already pervaded the parents' thinking, and it is difficult for them to take distance from it. It is not unusual for parents to present in these situations as having to walk on eggshells around their son or daughter. They will also describe scenes at home of the young person crying and becoming hysterical if challenged about how they see themselves and the problem, and even threatening to end their lives. The primary task then in this initial session is to provide containment for the parents and for their justifiable anxiety. Whilst not excluding medical and organic factors in the course of the assessment process, if we solely resort to an illness model we will foreclose on the meaning of the behaviour however complicated and threatening it appears to be. The Division of Clinical Psychology Guidelines refer to this as a potentially false assumption that the primary causal factor in the presentation of some mental disturbances is biological dysfunction, rather than understanding the behaviour as a response to complex life circumstances that need to be explored.

Creating a space for history taking

Seeing parents wherever possible together, before meeting with the young person, creates a space for the important history taking part of the assessment. It enables us to open up the history not only of the young person from birth, but also the history of the parents. We can make a reasonable assumption that human behaviour particularly when it is repetitive and disturbing as in the case of embedded problems, is never random. It is always connected within a dense interpersonal and familial matrix. For this reason in this initial assessment and formulation process, we make a hypothesis that the young person's behaviour however unusual, will tend to reflect very precisely the configurations of their own particular family. Not unlike a set of fingerprints, the embedded problem invariably reflects dysfunctional aspects of relational and family life that are specific, personal and characteristic only of that family.

Insight into the history of the young person is very important in helping us to understand how long the problem has been disturbing; whether it is of recent origin or whether the young person has displayed areas of vulnerability from an early age and in primary school. In this, the focus on the developmental task comes very much to the fore. We are also concerned with the parents' previous experience of childbearing and conception. We may find that there was severe illness in the parents, or a difficulty in conceiving, repeated miscarriages or a stillborn child. All this information constitutes important data about how the young person came into the family and what preceded their arrival. The very fact that there may have been serious difficulties in early or later childhood that were overlooked or denied by the parents, gives us important information about how the parents handle and respond to emotional challenges.

We may also find parents who initially offer a bland thin history of both their child as well as themselves. As we listen to the history, it becomes clear that the problem in the young person before it became embedded could have been attended to earlier, if there had been less denial on the part of one or both parents. In some cases a parent may brush off any concern about their son or daughter by describing their difficult behaviour as just part of their personality. As a result, this may have led them to overlook or put up with challenging behaviour. At other times parents may gloss over the problem by saying that the young person is exactly like themselves, as though this will put an end to the need for any further speculation about the origins of the problem, or indeed any need for help.

How the symptom is lived out in the family

Most importantly, what can be ascertained from the 'here and now' in the interaction with the parents in this first session? This may also throws light on the presenting problem. We may, for example, find an over-concerned and involved mother with her anxious and obsessive son, and a disengaged father. Or we may find an over-involved father with his daughter who makes himself her main confidante and excludes his wife from meaningful contact.

In summary, the presenting problem of embedded obsessive behaviour, whilst it is acknowledged as a serious problem for the young person, nevertheless still represents *the opportunity*. This necessitates that we do not become blinded by the symptom and then take action that would limit the therapeutic engagement and understanding of the problem. By persisting with the inclusion of the parents and giving time to the assessment, we begin the process of formulation that encompasses the inter-personal and systemic domains. By the end of this assessment meeting with the parents, we are in a position to offer a summary of what we have understood and begin to make even tentative connections between events, experiences and the young person's behaviour that will not have been evident hitherto to the parents. Making these connections, summarising and integrating what has been discussed, further provides containment for the parents, and sets the scene for the continuing therapeutic engagement with them, as well as with their son or daughter. What the behaviour may mean for the young person within the domain of the intra-psychic is described next.

The assessment and formulation process with the young person

There are two main elements that are important in carrying out the assessment and formulation process in therapeutic work with young people who present with obsessive worries. The first is that these problems should not be confronted head on as an apparently 'rational' way of eliminating the 'incorrect' belief whether about school performance, friendships or appearance. This rationalist approach will encounter strong resistance. Instead we need to understand that the problem with its attendant rituals is elaborately constructed largely as a defence mechanism, and has a distinct function for the young person. Sometimes it is helpful to explain that we would not expect them to give up the worry or the ritual, since we realise how much this means to them and how much they need it. This can be of great relief for the young person whose resistance to any therapy may be due to their worry that the therapist will try to wrest their convictions and core beliefs from them. In one such example, the therapist explained to a young girl with a number of body-based obsessive behaviours that she would not be asked to give these up knowing how important they were to her. In her response to this interestingly, the young girl expressed her wish to draw these behaviours or obsessive tics, which were connected with her face and body, so that she could thereby explain them to the therapist. Her drawings were extraordinarily detailed and vivid, and in the course of doing them and describing the behaviours to the therapist, it became apparent that she was already taking distance from them, and as a result she felt that they had less of a hold over her.

The second important element to keep in mind in the assessment and formulation process is that we are intent on finding the potential for health and growth within the young person. This places the focus on the person not the problem. Thus, the pitfalls of a bio-medical bias in interpreting the problem are avoided, which contribute to the trajectory of labelling the young person. In time-limited psychotherapy therefore, we are concerned with assessing *the capacity* of the young person from the outset and whether they are willing and able to work with us to gain a deeper understanding of their embedded problem. An advantage of time-limited therapy is that it enables us to make comments and pursue connections in a more direct way from the outset. This does not entail that we seek to correct the embedded view of the young person as 'incorrect' but that we offer some alternative ideas of why they may need to hold onto their particular beliefs. From a psychodynamic perspective we may speculate that many of these rigid and obsessive behaviours have their origin in an avoidance of aggression. Making this link and explaining to the young person why some people may be fearful of showing their anger helps to develop psychological mindedness. We should not underestimate the confusion that reigns amongst young people and their parents about why they feel the way they do. This has been referred to earlier as sharing the 'working machinery' of the psychodynamic process. It may also be described as psycho-education, which is considered as a legitimate component of therapeutic work.

Another effect of making this understanding explicit is that it gives permission for the young person to express these feelings perhaps for the first time. For example, a boy who was struggling with his need to promote perfectionism in all his work and activities, was able to express his rage at the way some of the boys behaved towards him in the classroom when they 'borrowed' his things and never returned them. He could not bring himself to be angry with them as this would disturb the perfect image of himself he was at pains to maintain. When this was discussed with the therapist, he could begin to understand that the need for him to control his anger was a dominating factor in his obsessive behaviour.

Part of assessing capacity in the adolescent and young person and their potential for health and growth, involves finding out about their lives beyond the presenting symptom. This refers to friendship, activities they enjoy and their hopes and ambitions for themselves. A capacity for a sense of humour is always a positive sign and can be a counterpoint to the sense of burdened persecution that often accompanies embedded problems.

The adolescent, the young person, the parents and the therapist

An important insight related to these embedded difficulties is that they are essentially family and relationship connected. This requires that the therapist makes this clear from the outset, so that the separate work with the adolescent/young person as well as with their parents is conducted in a transparent manner, understood and accepted by everyone involved. This allows the adolescent and young person to have time separately to air their views, grievances and fears and this is similarly available for the parents. At various times, the therapist may judge when it is appropriate to introduce joint meetings in which these separate 'understandings' can be brought together in the service of further expanding the work and any particular areas that need to be specifically addressed.

Helping parents to change the dynamic of the embedded problem

It is critical to involve parents because they will be the key change agents in helping to shift or totally eliminate the embedded problem. The old adage that we cannot change anyone else except ourselves, applies particularly well in this situation. Parents who have been struggling for some time to help their son or daughter will understandably perceive the problem as existing primarily *within* their child. As such, they will not have paid much attention to how their family dynamics have contributed to the problem and most importantly, how these dynamics continue to ensure that the problem remains cemented into the family structure. Many embedded problems have accompanying rituals with which parents and families comply for the sake of peace, or because of a fear that their son or daughter will become so enraged or fearful if they do not, that this will provoke an even worse situation for them. We may therefore hypothesise particularly with regard to obsessive behaviours that remain unchecked, that parents and often the whole family, are driven into 'servicing' the obsessive worry or conviction. This of course, not only shrivels the development of the adolescent and young person, but also shrivels the life of parents and family who fear that they must tread very carefully in any interactions with the young person. Treading carefully on eggshells creates the further problem of an illness discourse around the young person. This may have the function of shielding them from having to take a step back to understand their behaviour or to take any responsibility for it.

Resisting response to rituals

The role of parents therefore is critical in putting in place the first steps towards changing the dynamic of the household with respect to not continuing to service the needs of the embedded problem. An example of the way in which parents are dragooned into servicing the embedded problem is one parent, usually the mother, allowing herself to be monopolised to attend to the anxiety of the young person to the exclusion of other members of the family. It may also take the form of certain rituals that the family have to follow with respect to managing the anxiety of the young person, as well as having to respond to their repetitive questioning and excessive dependence. It has to be noted that these behaviours never succeed in allaying anxiety for the young person, and through their collusion with these demands, parents and families actually perpetuate and reinforce the belief and the anxiety. We hypothesise that because the young person feels that they are controlled by their anxiety, that they put their energies into trying to control the people around them. It is not unusual for the family in these situations to have become somewhat fragmented. Parents almost invariably become split and lose a sense of authority and cohesion. One parent is almost always drawn into a powerful and separate relationship with the young person to the exclusion of the other parent, which further weakens their capacity to work as a parenting team. On occasion, other members of the family such as siblings have been enjoined into the task of 'servicing' the obsessive behaviour which is also not conducive to their own positive development.

Making practical changes: Working together as a parenting team

As the therapeutic work progresses, we will have helped parents to gain some insight into how and why the embedded problem in the young person has arisen in the first instance, which is the prelude to their beginning to make practical changes within the household in not continuing to 'service' the problem. This involves supporting them to not respond to the usual demands of the young person, not to engage in any rituals and, to try to limit their angry and exasperated responses whilst holding firm. It is important to encourage parents to work together as a parenting team rather than for one parent to have to deal with the struggle while the other parent quietly creeps away. Helping parents to understand the developmental issues for the young person is crucial. We may hypothesise that the embedded problem has served to infantilise the adolescent and young person. The resulting anxiety and at times rigidity on their part, may have prohibited them from participating fully in social life with their peers. Classic Oedipal struggles are also at play here and in many cases represent a revival of earlier unresolved infantile experiences.

The parallel developmental task for parents

If we return to the focus on the developmental task and the promotion of health and growth in the adolescent and young person, then we may consider how this connects with their (unconscious) Oedipal struggle. We recognise that the developmental task for the child and adolescent has its parallel in the developmental task for parents. A critical task for parents as their children move into adolescence is to be able to successfully become a disappointment for them. Being a disappointment for adolescents and young people is the antithesis of maintaining a position of being in control and irreplaceable, as well as being the font of all wisdom for the present and into the future. It is not unusual to find that these issues are contributing factors to the anxiety and rigidities that are so typical of embedded problems in adolescents and young people. The anxieties and rigidities may at least in part be understood as the fear of the young person that they can never separate from one or both parents, and find a sense of self literally to stand up in. In many cases their continuing dependence and apparent gratitude to their parents is underpinned by an underlying sense of anger towards them and a wish to blame them for the hopelessness of their situation.

The impact of practical changes on the adolescent and young person

In time-limited psychotherapy where the method is the interactive model, the response of the young person to the change within the family dynamic is almost immediate. Once parents cease to service the obsessive behaviour and the rituals, this has a dual effect. Firstly, it opens up the possibility that the therapy with the young person can move beyond accepting the necessity of the behaviours and the rituals and hopefully begin to explore underlying issues that give rise to the behaviour. Secondly, by ceasing to service the behaviour, the parents become a disappointment for the young person and this helps them to begin to introduce more age appropriate expectations. Additionally for the young person, if the parents are a disappointment and no longer prepared to be involved in the rituals and the rigidities, it has the potential to force the young person to begin to look outside of the family, to friends and peers that had previously been disregarded. This fulfils the function of helping them move towards health and growth. Finally, despite their protestations about their parents and family ceasing to service their obsessive behaviour, the young person is given a message that their parents can provide a sense of safety and containment in other more appropriate ways.

It will be an inevitable part of the therapeutic process that this change in the family dynamic and the view of the embedded problem will make the adolescent and young person angry with their parents, who they will perceive as having broken a covenant with them about the 'need' for their problem to take centre stage in the family. They will also be angry with the therapist for having persuaded their parents to make these changes. It will not be unusual for the therapist to be dismissed and disparaged as unhelpful. Both of these responses should be viewed as an attempt to maintain the status quo and resist change. The strong emotions that emerge as a result are perceived as positive and a sign of capacity. As such, they can provide the leverage for a more dynamic therapeutic engagement rather than one in which the therapist becomes a kind of caretaker for the deadening obsessive behaviour.

Risks and reactions

This interactive approach taken in time-limited psychotherapy places demands on the therapist to be able to tolerate uncertainty and to manage risk. It is here that understanding the developmental task of adolescence enables us to recognise the challenges of transition for the young person and the fluidity of emotional states. We may hypothesise that the embedded behaviour represents an attempt at resolution about earlier and unresolved infantile and early childhood conflicts. By responding to the problem as the opportunity, and keeping the focus on health and growth, we have a greater chance of helping to untangle these conflicts, and enable them to become resolved before they become solidified in adult life. Since parents are the key to this process, we reconfigure the traditional one-to-one transference elements of the therapeutic process. The therapist's task in this interactive process is that of bringing about change to mobilise the development of the young person and open up and enhance the quality of their interaction and communication with their parents. As such, the therapist acts as facilitator, translator, connector and container.

Attention to the total field: The school setting

It is inevitable in working with adolescents and young people who present with embedded problems, that these problems cannot be contained within the family but overflow into school and other areas. Embedded problems such as severe anxiety, obsessive preoccupations and rigidities as they emerge in adolescence, cannot simply be dismissed as 'phases'. Many schools put in place good pastoral and counselling services to try to address these problems as best they can. When we take a dynamic view of the problem in which the different domains are connected, then we recognise that the core problem of anxiety within the young person overflows into the family as well as into the school community. Teachers and school counsellors need support and clarification to manage their anxiety so that they can work effectively with the young person in the school setting. For this reason dissolving of the therapeutic boundaries where the therapist with the consent of the patients, has explanatory meetings with the relevant staff, is particularly apposite and provides positive containment for all concerned. For the young person it also demonstrates the concern and support of the adults around them. For example a 14-year-old boy who had suffered from depression and crippling anxiety was unable to attend school for several months. As he made a slow recovery a decision was taken for him not to return to his old school at which he had been unhappy, but to commence at a different school. The therapist was concerned that no plan had been put in place about how he was going to literally cross the threshold on his first day. The therapist therefore worked with the parents and the school to ensure that he would be able to establish connections with key teaching and support staff as he entered the building and that they would be available to him to ensure he would successfully establish himself in this new environment.

The case management function

This case management function is intrinsic to the therapeutic task and is perceived as having equal therapeutic value to the contact with the patients. This returns us to ways in which we can manage risk for young people with embedded problems, which means that we must be particularly attuned to ways in which we can create connections and not disconnections between the therapy and the outside world in the best interests of the child and young person.

It is not unusual in these situations to find school staff and counsellors as anxious and paralysed as the parents and as worried about 'doing the wrong thing'. They may also be concerned about challenging the young person as well as the parents. Without revealing confidential information, it is possible to help school staff work out their own formulation of the problem, as it affects the young person within the school setting. Just as the parents are helped to use their authority in the home setting, the professionals in the school setting can be helped to be free to use their authority as it applies within the school. This may lead to shared meetings with the parents and with the young person when appropriate.

Consolidating health and growth

The outcome in therapeutic work with embedded problems is that the young person will feel more hopeful about themselves and will begin to look outwards beyond the rigid maintenance of their beliefs and rituals within the family towards the world of friendships and peer relationships. In other words they will become more interested in what everyone else is doing and want to be part of it. Here as well, the therapist has a role to play. Having withdrawn themselves from friendships, these young people may be concerned that they are not welcome in social groups at school, or that their peers dislike them, none of which may be true. Helping them to begin to make these reconnections is a gradual process. It often involves practical discussions and the giving of little tasks to help them reconnect. It is not surprising that young people who have become very dependent in the family, have never learned to use public transport so that they can get about and meet their friends. This in itself can become a shared task for the young person and their parents.

In conclusion, we recognise that assisting the young person and their parents to overcome embedded problems includes practical action and a capacity for reflection that draws attention to the dynamic interactive process that has at its core the promotion of health and growth.

Embedded problems in younger children

It is not unusual for younger children to present embedded problems in the form of phobias and high levels of anxiety. The focus on adolescent embedded problems referred to the ways in which these problems represent at least in part unresolved difficult earlier infantile and later childhood experiences. For younger children we may hypothesise that we are able to see these problems in the making, which gives us greater opportunities to intervene before they become encapsulated for the child and the parents.

The interactive nature of some of the more phobic elements of the behaviour of younger children with their parents is often visibly apparent. For example, an eight-year-old boy had developed a fear of death and had become convinced that his parents would die. He was worried about them when they went out and preferred that they all stayed at home. His interest in school and friendships had become affected. In this particular time-limited therapy, it was striking to hear from the meeting with the parents, how sudden shocking death and loss had permeated the mother's own life growing up. Her father had died suddenly without warning from a heart attack and following the funeral no more was spoken about him. His death was followed by two further accidental deaths of family members which were also never referred to. The mother's unresolved experience of mourning appeared to have become transmitted into her son as a petrified state of mind. We may speculate that the mother had made some mention of this without assuming that her son had actually heard what she said. However, this kind of intergenerational transmission of traumatic experience is not uncommon in families where the parents have not been able to mourn the loss of family members or metabolise the experience. In this case the validation for the mother in allowing her to acknowledge her traumatic history had the almost immediate effect of lifting the burden of responsibility from her son.

When the body speaks

However, there are other situations in which the parental conflict becomes internalised within the child to such an extent that it produces a physical response. This may take the form of the child experiencing physical pains for which no organic cause can be found. It may also take the form of regression to an earlier stage of development. The regression to soiling in an older child with a previously established history of toileting and no organic causation is one such example. It can become literally embedded in the child and may be very resistant to change. We may hypothesise that such a drastic physical regression has a meaning. It suggests that there is a communication that cannot be made verbally and that there is much that cannot be spoken of. That which cannot be spoken of therefore becomes subverted through the body and takes on a physical state of being, rather than becoming an emotional state of mind.

Taking a developmental stance provides a context for the consideration of problems that present themselves in the older child such as soiling. We know that young children under five years have to achieve mastery over the three key areas of feeding, sleeping and toileting almost all at the same time. Into this mix of course we add the beginnings of speech and communication. All of these tasks are dependent to a large extent on the co-regulating function with the parents as part of the interactive process. The readiness of children to achieve mastery in the areas of speech, toileting, feeding and sleeping, can be seen at least as dependent in part on the readiness of their parents to enable them to do so.

Developmental and task confusions

When the child experiences difficulties in achieving mastery in these different tasks, these become manifest in eating, sleeping and toileting problems. When they persist over time they are conceptualised as zonal, geographic and role confusions (Schmidt Neven, 2010). Zonal confusions occur primarily in relation to zones of the body that are concerned with eating and toileting. We may find parents over-preoccupied with the orifices of the child, with respect to what goes into one orifice, namely the mouth, and what comes out of the other, namely the anus. Geographical confusion is typified by sleeping difficulties when the child more or less permanently sleeps in the parent's bed whilst usually one parent sleeps in the child's bed. Role confusion is personified by the child who appears not to recognise any boundaries and when these are absent becomes confused about who is the parent and who is the child. It is not unusual for children to present problems in which all three confusions manifest themselves simultaneously, as they are all in a sense interconnected.

Emotional triggers

When faced with an embedded problem of incontinence in an older child we recognise that there are a number of emotional triggers for this state of affairs. When we take the developmental context into account we hypothesise that a function of the body, namely bowel movements and going to the toilet, has become appropriated in the service of another purpose. Being able to ascertain what this purpose may be is part of the therapeutic task in time-limited psychotherapy. The presenting problem is therefore perceived as the opportunity and given the dramatic nature of the symptom we can reasonably assume that it represents a reaction to the closing down of communication with important people in the child's life. The symptom of incontinence is particularly damaging for the child's growth and health and has an impact on schooling, learning and relationships as it literally shuts down engagement in a crucial developmental milestone. Time-limited therapy is then of considerable benefit as it enforces a sense of urgency both for the child as well as for the parents in attempting to solve the problem.

The interactive connection: Work with parents

From the interpretive perspective that an incontinence problem in an older child is literally a form of dammed up communication, it follows that taking an interactive parent and child-centred approach to the problem is critical. The parents' view of the cause of the problem and how they try to manage it is of specific interest as it is invariably connected. We may find parents who take an over-controlling and intrusive attitude towards their child and act as though the child's development is dependent on their actions. They believe that they are the ones who have to inform the child when to eat, and when to go to the toilet. In this way the parent's dominance has overridden the innate bodily cues of the child. The child therefore has ceased to listen to their own bodily cues and takes their cue about their bodies solely from their parents.

Where control is the dominant theme, we may find parents' preference for a strong medical response to the problem, even though no organic cause may be found. In these cases medical practitioners themselves may suggest an emotional basis for the problem. The extent to which parents may pursue medical investigation even though these may also be intrusive and uncomfortable for the child, gives us some indication of the lengths to which some parents may go to in order to avoid having to confront the emotional basis for their child's predicament. Given that the child is often encapsulated with the parents in the avoidance of the underlying reasons for the problem, they may be willing to go along with a medical approach which gives them the apparently 'safe' label of sick person and patient.

Emphasising health and growth

The task for the therapist is to make the health and growth of the child and the normalising of their development the central focus of the time-limited work. Communicating the urgency of this to the parents is central as the child cannot wait. This may involve challenging the parents' preferred medical patient label for the child. For example, in one such situation, parents had made a decision not to send their seven-year-old son to school once his incontinence had taken hold although this was not the recommendation of the medical professionals. By the time the therapist saw the child and parents he had missed a whole term of school and was understandably anxious about returning. He remained at home highly indulged by his parents and presented to the therapist as though he was in a kind of suspended animation, neither being part of the child world of school and peers, nor part of the adult world of his parents.

The therapist was emphatic that the child had to return to school at the earliest opportunity and much of the therapeutic work was concerned with the practical day-to-day arrangements of how the boy could be helped to manage his soiling if this occurred while at school. For the boy, this took the responsibility of managing his body away from the over-concerned control of his parents, and helped him to begin to develop some capacity instead, enhancing the beginning of his own body awareness.

Incontinence and ritualistic behaviour

Helping the parents to help the child is part of the process, particularly where as the embedded problem continues over time, it becomes associated with ritualistic behaviour. For some children incontinence takes the form of trying to resist their faeces coming out and holding on. At these times they become angry if their parents encourage them to go to the toilet. Parents may describe huge scenes in which at these times the child becomes rigid and controlling, demanding that the parents leave them or they may demand excessive reassurance about being loved.

Seeing both parents and taking a history of themselves and the child invariably reveals many complex issues. We may find that a child's incontinence is closely connected with the parents' highly acrimonious separation and their contradictory views of handling the situation. In the course of creating a formulation in these circumstances we may hypothesise that the child's incontinence may represent the only control they feel they have when everything else in their lives has become out of control. Maintaining a problem that is so resistant to help also functions to bring their parents together, and makes the child the central focus. It may also serve to distract the parents from fighting with each other. In these situations it is not uncommon for warring parents to become highly competitive with each other in their attempts to help the child. Their mutually contradictory views create further anxiety in the child and make the child less invested in giving up the problem behaviour.

It is not unusual as mentioned earlier for zonal confusions such as toileting problems to exist alongside geographical confusions such as sleeping problems, where the child is too frightened to sleep in their own bed and sleeps primarily with one or both parents. The overly involved parents may see this as further evidence of the child's need for them, and are happy to consider it as separation anxiety. However, it is more likely a further manifestation of the child's inability to develop a sense of their own identity through an appropriate separation from their parents.

The interactive connection: Work with the child

We may find in consultation with children who have experienced a lengthy period of incontinence that they present as being totally disengaged from their soiling problem, as though it exists completely out of their control and out of the control of their bodies as well as their minds. They may be pleasant and polite with the therapist but quite evasive. It may come as a surprise that they appear to be not very concerned or even embarrassed by the soiling problem which is a clear indication that its function is too important for them to readily give it up. From a developmental and meaning making perspective, the constant attention to their bodies combined in some cases with co-sleeping, recreates a revived infancy. This gives the child some temporary respite from their anxieties. This revived infancy may represent a time when things were happier for the child whether before parents divorced, or other difficulties occurred within the family.

Carrying the burden of family difficulties

When the move towards regressive behaviour is central to the problem, this often manifests itself in other aspects of the child's interaction. Having become separated from peers as well as the experience of learning if they are not attending school, children in the therapeutic setting may show a reluctance to engage with toys, drawing or fantasy play. They present as though the very core of their developmental process has been interrupted or arrested. In one case an intelligent seven-year-old girl with an entrenched soiling problem which had baffled the various professionals involved, drew pictures that evoked the kind of formless images of a much younger pre-school child. When asked to draw her family, these were represented as three heads with no bodies and these disembodied images in a blank white space seemed to capture the essence of her dilemma. The formlessness and emptiness of the drawing also suggests reluctance on the part of the child to reveal too much information.

A child whose separated parents were in permanent conflict eventually revealed that she was worried about having to take sides and seemed to have to put all her energies into maintaining a good relationship with each parent. However, she was aware that this was hard to do as she was always the person inbetween who also tried to stop the conflict between her parents.

We may also find where boys as well as girls carry a burden about parental and family difficulties that cannot be articulated, they also convey at times a world weary sense of wanting to bypass childhood altogether and arrive in adulthood as soon as possible. This may be demonstrated through the use of words and phrases that may have been picked up from the tense, angry and unhappy adults around them which they then repeat to the therapist in parrot fashion. These words and phrases referring to the breakdown of a parental relationship for example, such as 'these things happen' seem intended to provide the therapist with a kind of statement of fact that closes down communication. The child's world weary presentation is also conveyed in their reluctance to play with the toys, as though they have given up childish things a long time ago and are now more interested in the games and activities of adolescents or even adults.

Maintaining the momentum for change

We recognise that time is of the essence in helping the child move to health and growth and prevent the problem from becoming chronic with its attendant physical and psychological difficulties. By conveying directly to the child that we understand that they may not be able to speak in the usual way about things that are bothering them and that therefore their bottom has to do the talking, we let them know that there is a real meaning to what is happening that can be understood. It is also important to convey with the help of the parents that there is nothing physically wrong with the child's body, particularly when they have been involved in extensive medical investigations. These communications about the health of the child and the health and appropriate functioning of their body can be most helpfully carried out in a joint meeting with the parents and the therapist. This conveys that the parents are stepping out of a medical illness framework and can reassure the child that they can allow their body to do the work.

A successful outcome in helping the child is not only evident when the incontinence ceases, but can also become manifest in how they perceive their body. By helping the child understand that their body belongs to them, and to no one else, even their parents, helps them perhaps for the first time, to have a sense of ownership of and responsibility for their bodies. This has implications for their future personal and sexual interactions as they get older. The fact that they begin to have an awareness of ownership of their bodies also helps to create more age appropriate separation from their parents.

Reconnecting with development

The critical factor in time-limited psychotherapy with children with incontinence problems is to help them reconnect with normal development and to assist the parents and child together to move towards the instatement of health and growth. Given the need to find a quick solution to the problem in order not to further impede development, time-limited psychodynamic therapy has a helpful role to play. Placing the focus on the normalising of development, means that we need to make practical suggestions about the management of the problem as it manifests itself on a day-to-day basis. In this sense the practical is the personal, as the actions particularly of the parents, have an impact on perpetuating the problem or on helping to resolve it. Understanding the meaning of the symptom and exploring it as the opportunity, is a powerful element in achieving therapeutic success. Practical suggestions take the form of helping parents to contain their anxiety to help them cease their intrusive control and not to disrupt the functioning of their child's body. A position that emphasises health and growth and the child's own physical and psychological capacity takes precedence over a view of the child as ill, helpless and passive.

Helping parents to cease their participation in rituals is an important part of this process. This helps them to open up more appropriate avenues for caring and showing affection. Most importantly, it is vital to ensure that the child takes their place within the school community to enhance their capacity for learning and for developing peer and friendship contacts.

Widening the field

The impact of incontinence in a school-aged child has wide ramifications and is not something that can be kept hidden within the home. As a growing developing person, the child has connections with institutions within the wider world of which the school is the most significant. Reference has been made to the way in which soiling problems affect many areas of the child's life: cognitive capacity, learning and curiosity and friendship and peer relationships are all compromised. This is particularly troubling where children have missed a great deal of school due to the exclusive medicalisation of the problem. This is then combined with the parents' belief that the child will be unable or be too embarrassed to cope with demands of the school environment because of their incontinence. By expanding the therapeutic endeavour with the parents' agreement to include the school, we widen the support system for the child. In the first instance this ensures that the child continues to attend and is not held back from school. Secondly, we may find that school staff have long-standing experience with the many children in their care.

Working out a plan with the child, parents and the school about how the problem will be managed is part of the therapeutic endeavour. It gives a message to parents that they are not encouraged to come into the school specifically to attend to their child's soiling. It also gives the child a sense of responsibility in managing their own body and is often the point at which apparently sudden improvement takes place. As mentioned earlier we should not overlook how the incontinence problem has caused a developmental hiatus for the child and this may also affect their learning. If they have missed school and they are behind in their educational performance it makes it all the harder for them to want to return to school. The sensitivity of teachers in being able to recognise this problem is critical in making the school environment a place for the child where they can catch up on their learning and their friendships. School also provides a neutral haven for children who experience a high level of parental conflict.

Chapter 9

Empowering parents in times of change

It is not unusual for clinicians to find themselves concerned about aspects of parenting in the clinical setting that point to varying degrees of confusion on the part of parents about their parenting task and responsibilities. Confusions also arise when parents appear to have little idea of the physical and emotional milestones of their children's development. It is often these parental confusions that bring children and young people into the consulting room where the presenting problem is hard to disentangle given the fraught parent–child interaction.

It is a truism that we tend to believe that we live in changing times that are radically different and often worse than what has gone before. Our view tends towards a belief that the past was more innocent and less troubled or demanding overall. Whilst we would not want to view the past through rose-coloured glasses, we need to recognise that there have been major social and cultural changes in contemporary times. These changes have created fundamental alterations to the way we live now and these changes also have a major impact on how children are parented. At the start of the book the point was made that children, parents and families are at the tipping point of social change. This is inevitable, given the vulnerability of children and young people and their need for nurturance and support not only from their families but also from the wider community.

The impact of information technology

There are many factors that contribute to the difficulties that parents experience in current times. In Western societies these are to name a few: the lack of social cohesion and sense of community; the isolation of many parents; poverty and inequality; and the pressing need to maintain a livelihood in unstable economic times. However, some of the most radical changes to parenting have come from another source entirely, which is that of the explosion of information technology and the computer world. It is not simply the level and speed of communication that has been altered, but to a great extent how we think and feel, and how we conduct our relationships and the world we live in.

One of the most significant outcomes of this change is that children, young people and their parents for the first time, simultaneously have the same access to all the information that is available. This may be demonstrated by nothing more serious than the fact that children and their parents for the first time share their play interests together in the form of computer games. However, things go up a notch when both children and parents are involved in social media. The term 'natives' has been used to describe children who have been born into the age of information technology in contrast to their parents who have learned to use it in more recent times. This difference in itself is also significant as it gives children and young people a level of skill and capacity to control the information technology world beyond the ability of their parents and the adult world.

The flattening of hierarchy between children and their parents

One of the most significant implications of technological change and the fact that children and their parents share equal access to what it has to offer, is that it immediately flattens the established hierarchy between children and their parents. Whilst we may welcome a more open and democratic relationship between children, young people and their parents, the flattening of hierarchy leads in many cases to a blurring of the boundaries not only between children and parents, but also between how we define childhood and parenthood. In this context it is often difficult for parents to know where their authority and responsibility lie.

The flattening of hierarchy between children, young people and their parents is further encouraged by a marketing and advertising culture that is able to approach children and young people directly without first going through their parents. The expansion of the technological world enables them to do so, which further undermines the authority of parents. The fact that children and their parents may also be purchasing similar items such as clothing and games blurs the boundaries between childhood and adulthood even further. The apparent veneer of similarity between childhood and adulthood may also promote a sense of premature independence in children and young people which belies their dependence and their need for containment and nurturance.

What do children and young people need?

The paradox of the times we live in is that these factors do not in themselves change the essential nature of child development and the need of children and young people for positive attachments and protection. Frank Field (2010) a long-standing antipoverty campaigner has more recently shifted his concerns to what he observes as the poverty of child–parent relationships, and of 'how the home life of a minority – but worryingly, a growing minority of children – fails to express an unconditional commitment to the successful nurturing of children'. Field emphasises the need for attention to the early years of development, establishing parenting courses and support for parents, as well as placing 'parenting and life skills' into the school curriculum.

The problem of competing discourses about what children need is further described by Tom Billington (2006), a psychologist specialising in education, child protection and social and communication disorders. He identifies what he describes as competing discourses about the child and young person who is simultaneously perceived as being in need of protection and support as well as adult instruction, control and even punishment. His statement that 'frequently young people are now spoken of as if they were members of some kind of alien race from whom we have become totally disconnected...', may resonate with many clinicians who are confronted with the anger and confusion that parents express when they bring their children for therapeutic help.

The role of time-limited psychodynamic psychotherapy

The question then arises of what role time-limited psychodynamic psychotherapy can play in responding to this dilemma? The point has been made earlier that conventional treatments focusing primarily on the child will be unlikely to be effective in this changing and turbulent emotional and social landscape of childhood and parenthood. Equally, simply separating out therapy with parents without the child, may also not yield hoped-for outcomes. The fact is that children, young people and their parents are experiencing this level of change together, and therefore the interactive model has the potential to bring about positive therapeutic change. There is additionally a justified sense of urgency in needing to attend to these problems within a limited time frame to enable development, health and growth for the child and young person to continue unimpeded.

Identifying the three key elements that underpin child–parent conflict

Parents and children present to psychotherapists with problems of varying complexity. However, when we pare these down we find that what most of these problems have in common and what underpins many of these conflicts are the following three elements:

1   Confusion about the use of appropriate parental authority.
2   Blurring of boundaries between adults and children and the flattening of hierarchy.
3   Confusion on the part of parents and lack of understanding about the normal developmental milestones of children and young people.

In many situations these three elements combine and need to be taken into account in the therapeutic encounter with children, young people and their parents. The benefit of the time-limited model is that it is able to address these different elements more coherently, as it prioritises the duty of care and therefore an active and communicative approach. We recognise that some parents are genuinely confused about the need for boundaries, limit setting and the use of authority. Most will not have had any contact with a baby until they have had their own, and are simply not aware of what development entails. For this reason, the therapeutic approach necessarily needs to include what may be described as psycho-education in giving appropriate information about what children and young people need in order to grow and thrive. This does not involve handing out educational materials or reacting in a rigid or judgemental fashion, but is a legitimate part of the dynamic interchange of the therapeutic work as it unfolds.

Confusion about the use of authority and parental authority

One of the central confusions surrounding the use of authority is that many parents confuse having authority with being authoritarian. They may have grown up in aggressive or violent households in which their parents meted out arbitrary control, and they may have vowed never to repeat this with their own children. As a result they find themselves confused and shocked when their children override them and do not do as they are asked. Helping parents to recognise their own duty of care with respect to their children may at times have to be put plainly with respect to the actual rights and responsibilities invested in them, and that these cannot be avoided or divested. It is not unusual to find that when parents are confused about the authority invested in them, that they are also confused about how children learn to become socialised in the first place. Socialisation does not take place automatically as part of physical development, but is dependent on the co-regulatory relationship between the child and their parents that reflects their moment to moment, hour to hour and day to day interaction. We may be critical of parents who use electronic screens of all kinds as a babysitter and soother, but we may be surprised to discover how unaware they may be of how important they actually are to their children, and how much they matter to them.

For example, parents sought help for their four-year-old son following complaints about his behaviour from the kindergarten staff. The complaints concerned his high levels of aggression and difficulty in following instruction and cooperative play. The initial discussion with the parents revealed that both had different views of the problem. Whilst the mother was anxious and concerned, the father did not acknowledge that there was a problem. This fact in itself was immediately brought to the fore as the split between the parents made any intervention with their son ineffective. Moreover, the boy not unreasonably was led to believe that his father covertly gave him permission for his behaviour. The boy himself appeared compliant and eager to please with the therapist but looked wretched and miserable when his angry outbursts were discussed. Helping the parents to present as a united front and work as a parenting team to help their son formed the core of the work.

The use of therapeutic scaffolding

In using the term psycho-education we recognise that parents cannot simply proceed to make changes without the support of what may be described as the therapeutic scaffold. The therapeutic scaffold offered by the therapist in time-limited psychotherapy with parents, is represented by combining understanding of the meaning of behaviour and how it is enacted, with how a different pattern of behaviour can be established. For example, with respect to the four-year-old boy, it became clear that within their own home the boy did as he liked since his parents had never made clear to him what the rules of the household were. Helping the parents firstly to establish reasonable ground rules and then introduce them to their son, formed a part of creating this therapeutic scaffold. In these situations the focus is on helping the child to succeed and to find ways of managing their frustration, rather than to ignore the child and become angry when they act out. This involves helping the parents to be active and involved directly with their child and to begin to learn how to anticipate and prevent outbursts from happening, rather than conducting their parenting at arms length such as calling out for the child to stop an annoying activity when they are in a different room.

Blurring of boundaries and the flattening of hierarchy

It becomes difficult for parents to use their appropriate authority where the family dynamic is characterised by a blurring of boundaries about who is in charge. The flattening of hierarchy is often demonstrated through a stated or covert belief on the part of the parents that promoting a relationship of friendship between themselves and their children will be a way of avoiding conflict. Responsibility for who is in charge may shift from one family member to the other at any given time depending on who shouts the loudest. The sharing of experience in these families tends to be dominated by the sharing of electronic games and social media that eliminates the need for real personal and verbal interaction. In this context the parents themselves lose sight of their rights and responsibility as adults and become identified with the children. The need for the therapist to be clear about the impact this has on their parenting, and on the family dynamic, sets the scene for helping the parents make the shift to establishing basic boundaries. The challenge to the therapist can occur at various levels. For example, in one family meeting a father insisted he had only limited time available for his family because of the demands of his work. He pointedly placed his phone on the table in the course of the consultation where it gave off repeated although muted signals. This clearly conveyed the message that he was in huge demand and that he had more important business elsewhere. The therapist requested that he fully silence his phone for the purposes of the session, so that he would be less distracted and be able to give his full attention to what was being discussed.

In other cases, in the course of a consultation with the therapist, parents may complain about how hard it is to peel children off from their computer screens and games, whilst they themselves rush to look at their phones the moment there is a break in the discussion. These examples lead us to conclude that the excessive preoccupation with technology has not only led to the flattening of hierarchy between adults and children, but in some cases placed children low on the hierarchy in the minds of their parents. It will have become clear through the earlier discussion about finding the leverage in the parent–child interactive process, and extrapolating from the experience of the 'here and now' in the sessions, that these communications and observations cannot be ignored. Grappling with these observations and communications in a direct manner is part of the interactive and focused nature of time-limited therapeutic work.

The changing circumstances of parenting and the blurring of boundaries

The blurring of boundaries between parents and children also occurs through the changing circumstances of parents' lives through divorce, separation and bereavement. Single parents may find themselves plunged into situations where it becomes difficult to protect their children from the conflicts they experience with their ex-partners. These conflicts may be enacted in such an exposed manner that the child cannot escape from them and they are brought into the conflict by either or both parents who use them as confidantes. This manifests itself differently with boys and girls. Girls may find it easier to identify with their mothers although this also leads them into a parentified relationship where they feel that they have to take on a mothering role towards their mother. Boys struggle with a situation in which their longing for closeness with their mother is entangled with their fear of too much intimacy and dependence. The absence of a male role model often leads to their idealisation of the missing father and the denigration of the mother. Helping single parents to maintain a sense of separateness and not to lose sight of the continuing need to maintain their authority is part of this process. The children involved in these struggles may have been referred for a variety of problems some of them connected with psychosomatic conditions, while others, usually boys, are referred because of the escalating conflict with their mothers. This may bring to the fore partly unresolved Oedipal issues between the boy and his parents.

Empowering parents

In time-limited therapy helping the single parent to regain control of their parenting role is the first step in attending to the escalating aggression and conflict. Women in this situation often present as though ground down by their life circumstances and it is important to help them avoid a situation in which their sons in turn become identified in their minds with the role of aggressor. The active and communicative aspect of time-limited therapy plays a part in empowering the parent to take a stance that establishes her as a separate person as well as mother, without becoming over-involved and embroiled with her son. Without the help of a third party, mothers in this situation often become confused about where the boundary lies. This is associated with the guilt they feel about the suffering they believe has been inflicted on their son or daughter because of the conflict caused by the parental break-up. In one example of a conflictual relationship between mother and son, the boy stated that since his mother 'belonged' to him, he could treat her in any way he pleased.

Once single parents are helped to establish ground rules and have a greater conviction about the need for boundaries, then subsequent sessions with the mother and son together are helpful in explaining why these ground rules and boundaries have been put in place. This, in the majority of cases, results in relief on the part of the boy who can be free of the conflict that has been created by his parents.

Confusion about developmental milestones

It is important for therapists not to idealise the process of psychotherapy and not to perceive it as a golden space. In therapeutic work with children, young people and their parents, we need to take a robust and practical perspective not unlike the nature of development itself which is a work in progress. We may be confronted at times by the apparent lack of understanding on the part of parents about their child's development. Earlier the problem of pathologising the child was discussed, but we need to be equally cautious of not pathologising the parent when the real issue may be a genuine ignorance on their part.

There are a number of confusions that parents present about the developmental milestones of their children, starting virtually from birth when they expect the newborn infant to have an established sleep pattern. The problem of not recognising that children's behaviour has a meaning is almost universal right across the socio-economic stratum. In this regard children are generally perceived as having a kind of innate resilience that allows them to 'bounce back' from challenges as though they are rubber balls. The inclination towards encouraging premature independence is another confounding issue, particularly for the parents of adolescents. Most significantly, parents regularly undervalue their importance to their children and how their presence and communication is essential to their child's health and growth.

In time-limited psychodynamic therapy it is considered legitimate to address these confusions directly. When they are disregarded they invariably become an impediment to development and also lead to conflict and misunderstanding between parents and their children. The opening assessment process in which we explore the history of the child and young person and that of their parents, will already have given us an inkling of the nature of these dilemmas and what we may need to address.

Creating the therapeutic scaffold in this context means that we help parents to recognise the implications of their actions, and in some cases we have to challenge their assumptions about their children. For example, a family that had experienced a number of moves were considering a further change when their daughter had already demonstrated how difficult these transitions were for her. Her father insisted that she would never know the difference if they relocated, as children were not aware of their surroundings, and these things did not matter to young children. His statement created an opportunity to open up a conversation about change and transition and what this means for children in general and his daughter in particular. It also enabled us to be able to make connections between the changes that had already occurred in the family and the emotional problems his daughter presented.

Parenting young and older children

In working with children under five and their parents, this may involve the exploration of what parents can reasonably expect of their toddler and young child. We may find that this applies not only to having unrealistic expectations that are too high, but also to not having any expectations. For example, in a family in which preoccupations with the challenging behaviour of the older school child predominated, the younger three-year-old was treated like a baby, as though incapable of speech. Although the younger child was quite capable of speech, he had accommodated to his parents' low expectations by pointing and screaming for what he wanted or did not want, which created further tensions. The task of the therapist in these situations by being observant and active but not judgemental is to be able to bring a fresh perspective to how parents can meet their child's readiness for change.

The therapist's knowledge and understanding about the emotional milestones of development can be of great help to parents, such as taking a different view of why a child may be continuing to wet the bed long after they would have been expected to be toilet trained. Once we have ruled out any organic reason or emotional problem we may be struck by the fact that the parent describes the child as 'not being bothered' about wetting the bed which in itself gives us information about what is being accommodated and whether this is helpful to the child.

Transition for the adult and for the adolescent

In working with adolescents we may be struck by the way in which parents describe the problem they are experiencing with their son or daughter as though it is solely a function of the adolescent process itself. In other words, adolescence takes a lot of blame. However, our assessment may reveal that the problems presented have their origin in a much earlier age and stage and need to be understood as such. There are other examples where the move into adolescence on the part of the child arouses powerful but unrecognised emotions in the parent. This suggests that the point of transition for the adult may be as challenging as it is for the child. For example, a single parent who had been forced into taking on adult responsibilities as a young adolescent put her daughter into exactly the same position. The invitation into an adult world, while initially seductive and appealing to her young daughter, inevitably led to enormous conflict as it had effectively foreclosed on her need to be dependent and cared for by her mother.

Acknowledging the rightful place of hatred and aggression

As clinicians we recognise that many of the problems of concern to parents revolve around the aggressive behaviour or communication of their children. It is striking when this problem is presented that parents display a degree of shock and horror at the depth of negative feeling. Issues of aggression are also strongly connected with how parents manage authority and the setting of appropriate limits and boundaries. In a world in which children and young people are exposed every day to the aggression of adults through the media, their response takes us back to Billington's description of children and young people who are spoken of as though they are members of an alien race. However, it is in this area of helping parents to understand the task of aggression and hatred and how it can be managed, that psychodynamic psychotherapy can provide some of its greatest assistance.

It is of enormous benefit to explain to parents that aggression and hatred are important emotions that need to be negotiated by the child and young person as part of the normal developmental process. Helping children and young people negotiate this experience enables them to have a 'healthy hatred' in the service of developing inner resources. It is here that important connections are made between the child and the parents. The panic and fear that arises in parents may be understood in relation to their own family experience as well as the suppression of their own negative feelings. A typical example is that of parents who deny that their first born child has anything but total love for the new baby. Because they cannot allow for the rightful place of jealousy and rivalry, they become angry and disappointed when their older child slyly tries to hurt the newborn. By closing down any communication about what the child rightfully feels, this leads to the risk of anger and hatred going underground. It also leads to the child trying to split off the unpleasant and unacceptable part of themselves as though it belongs to someone else. The central theme of all therapy but particularly therapy that is engaged with child–parent relationships is that we try to open up communication about areas that are considered too dangerous to explore, of which hatred and aggression are central.

The therapeutic scaffold that provides the containment for parents enables these difficult and at times confronting issues to be addressed. Ultimately, time-limited psychotherapy through its active and interactive approach with children, young people and their parents, enables knowledge and understanding to be made available in such a manner that it becomes common knowledge in the crucial service of development and growth.

Chapter 10

The clinical outcome

Implications for training
and research

The end of the therapy and the clinical stance

The psychodynamic approach enables us to understand that human relationships are complex, and that there is rarely a neat ending to a problem, particularly where people have experienced trauma and challenges in their early lives. This implies that children, parents and young people may return for therapeutic help at a later stage, since some of these problems may not be fully resolved. As mentioned earlier, this is always a sign that the earlier therapy has been a success, and never that it has been a failure. In fact, the speed, with which people pick up the therapeutic process when they return, is in itself evidence of success and resonates with the earlier foundational work that has taken place.

This foundational work is underpinned by what may be described as the clinical stance of the therapist. In the context of our fast-paced environment, the clinical stance avers that there are no simple answers to the complexity of human experience and suffering. In seeking to find meaning and understanding, the clinical stance asserts that reflection is a legitimate part of this process and must always precede action. Maintaining the clinical stance is reassuring for clients and patients. It provides a containing framework for them, as opposed to one which seeks after facile solutions, and is not dependent on the nurturing of relationships.

How do we evaluate change? The place of the review

Psychodynamic work is essentially attuned to understanding the repetition of unhelpful actions and practices that impede development both for adults and children. Although the 'working through' of these experiences takes place over a shorter period of time than in conventional open-ended therapy, the intensity of the time-limited process can in itself be helpful. The sense of urgency that often accompanies the problems of the child and young person, gives time-limited psychodynamic psychotherapy its impetus in working towards solutions, which whilst they may not attend to the full panoply of problems, can go a considerable way to unlocking the impediments to development. Luborksky (1984) refers to this as helping patients gain a greater level of mastery over their relationship difficulties.

The best way to evaluate change is to ask the client or patient. Even time-limited psychotherapy should build in a review halfway through the therapy for everyone concerned. Reviewing the therapeutic progress has an important function in all psychotherapy as it offers a space in which both therapist and patient temporarily step out of 'role' for a brief period of time in order to review the therapeutic work. We often ignore the fact that psychotherapy comprises the (often) tacit acceptance of the 'role' of patient and the 'role' of therapist as a given, which may be rarely or never referred to in traditional open ended therapy after the first session.

It is postulated that a level of transparency and the need to step out of 'role' in order to review the therapy, should be an essential element of any therapy of whatever length. The absence of a review goes some way to explaining the at times confused sense some patients have even after many years of therapy, about what has actually been achieved. The lack of review may be justified by the rationalisation that everything the patient produces has a pathological and/or unconscious intent, and therefore cannot be open to everyday life scrutiny, and is only to be considered within the context of the transference. It is here that psychotherapists may end up being hoisted on their own petard. Patients may then have to resort to acting out through coming late, missing sessions, or abruptly terminating the therapy, because they have never been able to have a conversation with their therapist about where they are going, when they may arrive at their destination, and what the outcome might be.

The place of the double task

The organisational consultant and psychoanalyst Harold Bridger (1990) has described the process of building in a review as 'the double task'. He states that all organisations need to carry out a dual task; the first of which is to carry out the task and do the work, and the second is to review the task. The process of review is essential to assessing the continued relevance of the work, including what changes need to take place. Time-limited psychotherapy with children, parents and young people if it is to be a dynamically alive process committed to change, must do the same.

The review offers the opportunity to re-address the formulation that was made at the outset of the therapy. By carrying out a review, one is not advocating trying to please the patient or client, or pull up the roots of the therapy to see how it is growing. Rather, it is a process that acknowledges that children, parents and young people have come into therapy because of a genuine desire for change and improvement in their emotional and relational circumstances. It follows that they can be trusted to engage in a review halfway through the therapy, in order to evaluate how things have gone, and what needs to be attended to in the next part of the therapy. Stepping back into 'role' for both the therapist and patients, following the review, becomes an accepted part of the process because of the relationship of trust that has been established, that enhances the therapeutic alliance and anchors the therapy.

Carrying out the review in the spirit of Bridger's 'double task' should not be confused with some of the current directives in some government-run child and family mental health services, to check the usefulness of each session with the patient, whether child, adolescent or adult, at the end of each session. We would be advised to be cautious about such a directive which constitutes a commodification of the therapeutic relationship, under the guise of democratic participation. Our understanding of the transference elements in the therapeutic relationship, as well as sheer common sense, would inform us that the therapeutic engagement can have its ups and downs, and that the overcoming of resistance is one of the most significant challenges in therapeutic work. Additionally, the fact that therapy is time-limited does not in any way detract from, or minimise our attention to the sense of continuity that is intrinsic to the process.

Assessing therapeutic outcome

When it comes to assessing therapeutic outcome Emanuel *et al.* (2013) are unambiguous about the need for child psychotherapists to find ways of monitoring and describing outcomes for psychotherapy, if child psychotherapy is to remain an integral part of the UK National Health Service. They warn that the UK government's focus on monitoring outcomes reflects 'a much wider international consensus' and is therefore a necessity. Emanuel *et al.* report on the use of the Goal-Based Outcomes Measure (Law and Jacob, 2015) within a metropolitan hospital-based child and adolescent mental health service. The authors contend that the use of an aim-based measure does not determine the progress of therapy and what must be discussed.

Rather, it creates an opportunity to explore why the patient or family has come into treatment and what they (and the therapist) hope to achieve. Emanuel *et al.* describe this as a flexible and helpful process that creates a 'triangulation of information and understanding'. This 'triangulation of information' reflects a collaborative endeavour in which information is gathered from the patients as well as from other professionals working within the multi-disciplinary service. The experience of using the outcome measure is also perceived as throwing light in turn, on some of the complexities of the therapeutic process.

What constitutes a positive outcome?

A positive outcome in time-limited psychodynamic psychotherapy would lead to the following changes:

- Reframing the symptom or presenting problem of the child and young person as having meaning, and thereby opening up communication between them and their parents or caregivers;
- Creating a reflective communication process that promotes resilience for the future;
- Supporting the child and young person to 'find their real voice' and supporting parents to 'find their own voice';
- Supporting parents' own knowledge to 'own what they know' and assume appropriate authority.

Reframing the meaning of the symptom

As discussed throughout the book, the aim of the therapeutic work with children and young people is to give their presenting problems its rightful place and legitimacy. Our understanding is predicated on the assumption that in the vast majority of cases, the child or young person has to resort to annoying, worrying or challenging behaviour because no other avenue of communication is open to them at that particular moment in time. This is powerfully described in Bowlby's classic 1979 paper, 'On knowing what you are not supposed to know and feeling what you are not supposed to feel'. Once we understand that difficult behaviour may be a code for what cannot be expressed in another way, we can begin to address why this may be so, and facilitate the process of opening up the 'real' communication that needs to take place between the child, young person and their parents. A relationship and meaning making therapeutic process in which children and young people are perceived as reliable witnesses to their own experience, minimises the need for acting out and dysfunctional behaviour. It has the further advantage of enabling children and young people to 'find their own voice' and to 'give voice' to their own experience, which in turn promotes their capacity for self-regulation.

Creating a reflective process to promote long-term resilience

The outcome of a meaning making and relationship-centred approach as opposed to simply giving strategies is that a process is set in motion that can be utilised by everyone long after they have ceased to be in contact with the therapist. We make an assumption that the reflective process becomes internalised by the children, young people and parents, thereby providing them with a more permanent model of how to respond to future problems. Thus the process of stepping back, of not immediately accepting that what you see is what you get, and creating a hypothesis about what may be happening, is a method that is eminently transportable for children, young people and their parents.

Supporting parents to assume authority and 'own' what they know

Clinical evidence indicates that programmes and therapy that empower parents to think for themselves, and articulate their needs, in the long term provide the best outcomes for children (Miller and Sambell, 2003). A problematic recurring theme of contemporary parenting in this regard relates to parents' confusion about how and when to assert their authority. Parents typically confuse the use of authority with being authoritarian, which leads to extremes in either being too permissive or too controlling. A good outcome of time-limited psychotherapy is one in which parents' authority is instated, as well as their ability to work as a parenting team. Supporting parents to 'own' what they know, further acknowledges and capitalises on, the real inherent knowledge that parents have about their children, setting them to make use of this knowledge on an ongoing basis.

Chapter 11

Shifting the paradigm towards positive mental health for children, parents and young people

Revisiting research: Making it meaningful

This book asserts that there is a need for an urgent paradigm shift in how we conduct research into time-limited psychotherapy. This is not solely a concern of child psychotherapists, but also of the larger professional group of mental health practitioners. As mentioned earlier, the British Psychological Society presented a challenge to the authors of the DSM (V) (American Psychiatric Association, 2013), criticising the predominant 'medicalisation' disease model of distress in both children and adults. As part of creating a paradigm shift, we must be clear about who the beneficiaries are of research that follows a symptom-based medicalised model that exclusively utilises the randomised controlled trial. We need to ask questions about whether the 'evidence' thereby derived, is ultimately in the best interests of children and young people.

The role of professionals themselves is an important part of this inquiry. In research carried out to ascertain how professionals construct the mental health problems of children, parents and families (Schmidt Neven, 2008), it was striking to discover a *professional as victim discourse* that ran like a leitmotif through all the interviews with the professionals. Whilst the *professional as victim discourse* was understandably strong in those professional groups with the least amount of discretion in managing their caseloads, and their day-to-day work, it was particularly evident in one of the most powerful groups interviewed, namely the psychiatrists. They perceived themselves as the victims not only of the demands of the organisations they worked for, but also of the broader constituency of opinion-shaping journals, particularly in the United States. This was given as the major justification for example, for taking a narrow research focus that favoured the randomised controlled trial. The psychiatrists also perceived themselves as the victims of a community that forced them into over-diagnosis and prescription, and as such, they perceived themselves additionally as being at the mercy of society's demands and expectations.

This kind of self-referential discourse and the maintenance of the status quo is intrinsic to many professional groups. However, it is particularly disturbing where professionals have responsibility for the mental health and wellbeing of children and young people. We may question therefore whether we can reconcile conducting research to justify professional relevance, with promoting findings that have relevance for our patients.

Research and restating our duty of care

The complaint from professionals that they are victims of the prevailing bio-behavioural paradigm, and therefore are powerless to create change, cannot be considered acceptable in the light of the duty of care we hold towards children, young people and their parents. Our duty of care runs in parallel with the professional role of advocate, and takes a values-based approach that supports the rights of the child and young person. Professionals in child and family mental health including child psychotherapists, therefore need to become emboldened to take action to bring about a paradigm shift, particularly with respect to promoting meaningful research that has tangible outcomes. Policy does not constitute a tablet of stone, but is there to be engaged with, opened up and exposed to criticism. We need to lobby and inform policy makers and politicians, that narrowing the theoretical and research perspectives in which we consider services for children and young people, is ultimately counter-productive and damaging to them.

Doing research differently

The main argument against the exclusive use of the traditional randomised controlled trial is that it is a poor fit with the type of inquiry that is needed to elucidate how we may best approach the psychological and emotional problems of children, parents and young people, and how we may contribute to their overall wellbeing. The main reason for this is that the randomised controlled trial transposes a model used in the exact sciences, to an area that is subject to human experience and multiple variables. The attempts to reduce this complexity to the identification of one variable, such as clinical depression, within a research inquiry, will always produce less than hoped for outcomes. Practitioners in child and adolescent mental health are particularly vulnerable in this regard, as in a cost-cutting climate there is a tendency to conflate professional status and professional relevance, with treating the most disturbed children and young people. This appears to go hand in hand with the assumption of a reductionist approach that justifies the use of the randomised controlled trial in researching and treating problems such as depression.

In this sense, the single identifiable variable becomes in the terms of philosopher Immanuel Kant, 'the thing in itself' which can be neither confirmed nor denied or scientifically demonstrated. The philosopher and educationalist John Dewey (1950) argues against the use of dogma and absolutism in the way in which we construct theory and understanding, as this leads to the emergence of 'hard and fast opposites'. Instead Dewey calls for a flexible approach based on the creation and testing of hypotheses that can be worked on, rejected and expanded, to accommodate the experience of our changing needs and requirements.

From this we may infer that we will gather the most useful information from an approach to research that explores the 'lived experience' of people, and how they attribute meaning to their experience. This phenomenological perspective that utilises qualitatitive analysis is more likely to produce what in research terms is called 'thick' data. 'Thick' data are by their very nature multi-dimensional as opposed to being one-dimensional. An interpretivist analysis of such data as Glesne and Peshkin point out, is 'filled with multiple, often conflicting meanings and interpretations. The interpretivist researcher attempts to capture the core of these meanings and contradictions' (Glesne and Peshkin, 1992, p.19). Here we come full circle with Shedler's (2006) description of the psychoanalytic enterprise as contributing a vocabulary with which to explore inner contradiction. A time-limited approach to psychodynamic psychotherapy with children, parents and young people, opens up a range of possibilities that would lend itself particularly well to relevant research inquiries. These would, in Shedler's terms, enable us to explore a wider range of phenomena that are affected by the therapy. Certainly a broader conceptual research framework would immediately lift the burden of the pathology based labelling for children and young people.

The research possibilities that arise from time-limited psychodynamic psychotherapy may be summarised as follows:

- Research that examines what constitutes the essential inter-relationship between parents and children and young people, and how this contributes to therapeutic outcome in time-limited psychotherapy;
- Research that explores the views of parents about time-limited therapy and the kind of time frame they find most helpful;

- Research that engages directly with children and young people as legitimate informants about their experience, and explores their views of their problem and the therapy;
- Research that examines the enormous capacity for growth and self-healing in the child and young person, and how this resource may be harnessed in ways that will contribute to positive outcomes in time-limited therapy.

Being at the forefront of prevention

One of the main arguments of this book is that practitioners in child and adolescent mental health in relation to relevant research should primarily be concerned with prevention. The key question to ask is how the various disturbances and problems in children and young people have arisen in the first instance. Child psychotherapists and other professionals who work with children and young people, through their training and experience are in a particularly good position to attempt to address this question of inquiry through the use of qualitative research. Qualitative research that is predicated on psychodynamic understanding has the potential to have an impact at the policy making and political level if it is clearly articulated. Other researchers in the field such as Miller (1997), point to the capacity of qualitative research to 'develop analytic perspectives that speak directly to the practical circumstances and processes of everyday life' (p.24). It is worth noting in this respect, that both psychodynamic psychotherapy as well as psychoanalysis are interpretive disciplines.

It is also interesting to note that the relatively new area of translational research proposed by the American National Institutes of Health (NIH), is very much concerned with research that speaks directly to the practical circumstances and processes of everyday life. The sense of urgency of translating research and knowledge findings from the laboratory to the public sphere, has its parallel in exploring ways in which our existing clinical and research knowledge can be translated into effective services for children and young people as they 'cannot wait'.

Translational research is concerned with the fostering of 'the multidirectional and multidisciplinary integration of basic research, patient-oriented research, and population-based research, with the long-term aim of improving the health of the public' (Rubio et al., 2011, p.2). Rubio et al. refer to the terms of reference of the NIH which includes attention to research that is concerned with adopting best practice (my italics) in different community settings. The cost-effectiveness of treatment and prevention is another area of interest for inquiry and further research.

Translational research as a relatively new methodology is particularly concerned with the adoption of a multi-disciplinary approach that is predicated on the sharing of knowledge across boundaries. The multi-disciplinary collaboration that is at its core, could be well applied in a model of time-limited psychodynamic psychotherapy which takes as its starting point the need to *widen the total field* in work with children, young people and their parents. Creating research linkages between the therapeutic work, and the child and young person's school experience, for example, could be one such possibility. The impact of this type of community-based research is described by O'Fallon and Dearry (2002) in the context of addressing environmental health concerns that involve a partnership between academic investigators and community members to promote prevention. Whilst much of the focus of translational research has been on physical health, Steven Woolf (2008) has argued for a much wider definition to include other relevant knowledge including that of psychology, to improve health outcomes and promote the quality of life. Utilising the extraordinary body of psychodynamic knowledge and information about child development and family functioning, could make a highly relevant contribution to broadening of the field of research and inquiry. This is of particular relevance with regard to our understanding of the aetiology of child and adolescent psychological problems.

Training for the future

What kind of training would be most appropriate in time-limited psychotherapy for those child psychotherapists, child psychologists and other professionals who are committed to a psychodynamic approach in working with children, young people and their parents? The model of time-limited psychodynamic psychotherapy proposed in this book is essentially an integrated interactive one, in which the problem, its context and its solution is viewed as all one piece. This makes particular demands on the practitioner and also challenges contemporary approaches to child and adolescent mental health services, which are often fragmented or heavily focused on the individual to the exclusion of the context. Involving parents actively in the therapeutic work is a critical part of this training. Therefore, practitioners in time-limited psychodynamic psychotherapy need to be as proficient in working with parents and adults as they are with children and young people. The model of time-limited psychodynamic psychotherapy is not one that merely informs parents solely as onlookers, but has them engaged in their child's therapy.

Training for time-limited psychodynamic psychotherapy is best considered within a framework that is concerned with developing best practice in the field and with the wide dissemination of this best practice within the professional community. Best practice in the context of time-limited psychotherapy is predicated on a refreshed and recalibrated conceptualisation of what is essentially constituted by a psychodynamic approach, particularly in work with children and young people. This means that training institutions need to move beyond representing one or other psychoanalytic pioneer of the past. Their primary task is to ensure that trainees have the best access to current knowledge and information, and are able thereby to hone a critical attitude to examining this information at the broadest level.

Training practitioners in time-limited psychodynamic psychotherapy entails working with and attending to *the total field* that surrounds the child and adolescent. Incorporating the *total field* enables us to assess and focus on *identifying and promoting capacity*. This does not imply that psychotherapists must abandon their core therapeutic task. However, they must be trained to be cognisant of the complexity of the dynamics that surround the child and young person, and how these not only inform, but also perpetuate the presenting problem. These complex dynamics are not static but will change over time.

Training practitioners to engage effectively where appropriate with the networks that surround the child and young person, has a threefold function. By widening the field of inquiry, this often leads to shortening the length of therapeutic involvement. Second, it creates a stance that links psychotherapy with advocacy, and provides necessary containment for the child and young person. Third, through the broadening of the therapeutic process, psychological mindedness is promoted in collaboration with other professionals and the community that surrounds the child.

Whilst it is important for practitioners to have a sound understanding of psychopathology, training in time-limited psychotherapy introduces an additional health and wellbeing dimension to therapeutic practice. The skill building required for this type of practice involves to some extent a reversal of conventional practice, so that the presenting symptom is not viewed as the problem but as *the opportunity*. Training in time-limited psychodynamic psychotherapy is further grounded in the acknowledgement of the inherent capacity within the child and young person, for growth and change.

It was stated at the outset, that acknowledging the value of the previous work and professional experience of trainees is important in promoting a more three-dimensional experience of training. Many of the psychotherapy training courses already exist at postgraduate level, where students come into these trainings often with a wealth of previous experience. It is this experience and exposure to a wide range of emotional and psychological problems of children and young people, that will be most helpful to the development of professional skills in time-limited psychotherapy, rather than solely their experience of long-term psychotherapy.

In addition to this, there is the need to expand the contact that trainees have with professionals from related disciplines in the course of their training. Understanding of the total field is enriched by learning about the wider social, organisational and cultural contexts of the children and parents who come into therapy. The need to create strategic links and alliances with other professionals is a vital part of this training process. These collaborative links are particularly important in trying to help children and adolescents with complex inter-generational problems, where no single practitioner or single treatment, is realistically going to create significant change.

This view resonates with psychoanalyst Otto Kernberg's (2014) recommendations for innovation in psychoanalytic education. He makes the point that we need to be cognisant and inclusive of approaches and scholarship that lie on the boundary of our professional work. For Kernberg these include evolutionary and developmental psychology, experimental and social psychology, as well as sociology and cultural anthropology. Ultimately, connecting psychodynamic understanding within the wider field of scholarship in related fields will be the most effective way of ensuring its continued relevance in the context of mental health care.

Combining practice, training and research

Training in time-limited psychodynamic psychotherapy encourages the promotion of specialists in the field who can in turn disseminate information and skill building to further generations of psychotherapists. It lends itself particularly well to combining training with a variety of clinical research inquiries. These research inquiries necessarily open up a new field that is concerned with prevention and that examines the aetiology of emotional and psychological problems of children and young people within a broader relational and social context. Finally, a confluence of training and research that turns the lens onto the children and young people themselves, and gives them a voice, has the great potential to incorporate their contributions to inform the future development of time-limited psychodynamic psychotherapy.

Bibliography

Abbass, A., Hancock, J., Henderson, J. and Kisely, S. (2006). Short-term psychodynamic psychotherapies for common mental disorders. *Cochrane Database of Systematic Reviews*, Art. No. CD004687.

Abbass, A., Town, J. and Driessen, E. (2012). Intensive short-term dynamic psychotherapy: A systematic review and meta-analysis of outcome research. *Harvard Review of Psychiatry* 20(2):97–108.

Abbass, A.A., Raburg, S., Leichsenring, F., Refseth, J.S. and Midgley, N. (2013). Psychodynamic psychotherapy for children and adolescents: A meta-analysis of short-term psychodynamic models. *Journal of the American Academy of Child and Adolescent Psychiatry* 52(8):863–75.

Ackerman, N. (1966). *Treating the Troubled Family*. New York: Basic Books.

American Psychiatric Association. (2013). *Diagnostic and Statistical Manual of Mental Disorders*, 5th edn. Washington, DC: APA.

Balint, M. (1964, reprinted 1986). *The Doctor, his Patient and the Illness*, 2nd edn. London: Pitman Medical; originally published in 1957, by Churchill Livingstone.

Bateman, A. and Fonagy, P. (2008). The development of borderline personality disorder: A mentalising model. *Journal of Personality Disorders* 22(1):4–21.

Bateman, A. and Fonagy, P. (2013). Mentalisation-based treatment. *Psychoanalytic Inquiry* 33(6):595–613.

Bateson, G. (1973). *Steps to an Ecology of Mind*. London: Paladin.

Bellis, M.A., Lowey, H., Leckenby, N., Huges, K. and Harrison, D. (2014). Adverse childhood experiences: Retrospective study to determine their impact on adult health behaviours and health outcomes in a U.K. population. *Journal of Public Health* 36(1):81–91.

Bentall, R.P. (2009). *Doctoring the Mind: Is our Current Treatment of Mental Illness Really Any Good?* New York: New York University Press.

Bentall, R.P., Wickham, S., Shevlin, M. and Varese, F. (2012). Do specific early-life adversities lead to specific symptoms of psychosis? A study from the 2007 The Adult Psychiatric Morbidity Survey. *Schizophrenia Bulletin* 38(4):734–40.

Bevington, D., Fuggle, P., Fonagy, P., Target, M. and Asen, E. (2013). Innovations in practice: Adolescent mentalisation-based integrative therapy (AMBIT): A new integrated approach to working with the most hard to reach adolescents with severe complex mental health needs. *Child and Adolescent Mental Health* 18(1):46–51.

Billington, T. (2006). *Working with Children: Assessment, Representation and Intervention.* London: Sage Publishing.

Bion, W.R. (1962). *Learning from Experience.* London: Heinemann.

Bowlby, J. (1949). The study and reduction of group tensions in the family. *Human Relations* (2):123.

Bowlby, J. (1973a). *Attachment.* Harmondsworth: Penguin.

Bowlby, J. (1973b). *Separation.* Harmondsworth: Penguin.

Bowlby, J. (1973c). *Loss.* Harmondsworth: Penguin

Bowlby, J. (1979). On knowing what you are not supposed to know and feeling what you are not supposed to feel. *Canadian Journal of Psychiatry* 24:403–408.

Bowlby, J. (1988). *A Secure Base: Clinical Implications of Attachment Theory.* London: Routledge.

Bridger, H. (1990). Courses and working conferences as transitional learning institutions. In: Trist, E. and Murray, H. (eds). *The Social Engagement of Social Science: The Socio-Psychological Perspective,* vol. 1. London: Free Association Books.

Briggs, A. and Lyon L. (2012). Time-limited psychodynamic psychotherapy for adolescents and young adults. In: Lemma, A. (ed.) *Contemporary Developments in Adult and Young Adult Therapy: The Work of the Tavistock and Portman Clinics.* London: Karnac.

British Psychological Society: Division of Clinical Psychology (2011). *Good Practice Guidelines for the Use of Psychological Formulation.* Leicester: BPS.

British Psychological Society: Division of Clinical Psychology (2013). Position statement on the classification of behaviour and experience in relation to functional psychiatric diagnosis: Time for a paradigm shift. *British Psychological Society,* May, 2013.

Burck, C., Barratt, S. and Kavner, E. (2013). *Positions and Polarities in Contemporary Systemic Practice: The Legacy of David Campbell.* London: Karnac Books, Thinking and Practice Series.

Byng-Hall, J. (1991). An appreciation of John Bowlby: His significance for family therapy. *Journal of Family Therapy* (13):5–16.

Campbell, D., Bianco, V., Dowling, E., Goldberg, H., McNab, S. and Pentecost, D. (2003). Family therapy for childhood depression: Researching significant moments. *Journal of Family Therapy* 25(4):417–35.

Clulow, C. (ed.) (2001). *Adult Attachment and Couple Psychotherapy.* London: Brunner-Routledge; Taylor and Francis.

Clulow, C. (1997). *Partners Becoming Parents.* Lanham, MD: Jason Aronson.

Cowan, P.A., Cowan, C.P., Pruett, M.K., Pruett, K. and Wong, J. (2009). Promoting fathers' engagement with children: Preventive interventions for low-income families. *Journal of Marriage and Family* 71(3):663–79.

Cowan, P.A. and Cowan, C.P. (2014). Controversies in couple relationship education (CRE): Overlooked evidence and implications for research and policy. *Psychology Public Policy and Law* 20(4):361–83.

Cowan, P.A. and Cowan, C.P. (2015). Focus on the co-parenting couple: A new approach to encouraging father involvement and strengthening parent–child relationships. *International Journal of Birth and Parent Education* 2(3):31–35.

Davanloo, H. (2005). Intensive short-term dynamic psychotherapy. In: *Kaplan and Sadock's Comprehensive Textbook of Psychiatry.* Kaplan, B.J. and Kaplan, V.A. (eds). New York: Lippincott Williams and Wilkie.

de Shazer, S. (1988). *Clues: Investigating Solutions in Brief Therapy.* New York: W.W. Norton.

Dewey, J. (1899). In: *Psychology Misdirected.* Sarason, S.B. (1981). New York: Free Press.

Dewey, J. (1950). In: Lindeman, E.C. (ed.) *Reconstruction in Philosophy.* The New American Library: A Mentor Book.

Dolan, J.G. (2008). Shared decision-making transforming-research into practice: The Analytic Hierarchy Process (AHP). *Patient Education and Counselling* 73:418–25.

Edwards, J. and Maltby, J. (1998). Holding the child in mind: Work with parents and families in a consultation service. *Journal of Child Psychotherapy* 24(1):109–33.

Emanuel, R., Catty, J., Anscombe, E., Cantle, A. and Muller, H. (2013). Implementing an aim-based outcome measure in psychotherapy service. Published online 9 May 2013, *Clinical Child Psychology Psychiatry.* DOI: 10.1177/1359104513485081.

Field, F. (2010). *The Foundation Years: Preventing poor children from becoming poor adults.* London: HM Government.

Glesne, C. and Peshkin, A. (1992). *Becoming Qualitative Researchers. An Introduction.* White Plains, NY: Longman.

Goldberg, S. (2000). *Attachment and Development.* Texts in Developmental Psychology Series. London: Arnold.

Good, B. and Kleinman, A. (1985). In: Kleinman, A. and Good, B. (eds). *Culture and Depression: Studies in the Anthropology and Cross-Cultural Psychiatry of Affect and Disorder.* Berkeley and Los Angeles: University of California Press.

Goodyer, I. (2014). *From phenotypes to therapeutics: Sub-typing depressed youth to aid treatment success and be ready for treatment failure.* Address given to the 21st World Congress of IACAPAP, 11–15 August, Durban: South Africa.

Goodyer, I. *et al.* (2011). Improving mood with psychoanalytic and cognitive therapies (IMPACT): A pragmatic effectiveness superiority trial to investigate whether specialised psychological treatment reduces the risk for relapse in adolescents with moderate to severe unipolar depression; Study protocol for a randomised controlled trial. *Trials* (12):175.

Harold, G.T. and Leve, L. (2012). Parents and Partners: How the parental relationship affects children's psychological development. In: Balfour, A., Morgan, M. and Vincent, C. (eds). *How Couple Relationships Shape our World: Clinical Practice, Research and Policy Perspectives.* London: Karnac.

Havighurst, S.S. and Downey, L. (2009). Clinical reasoning for child and adolescent mental health practitioners: The mindful formulation. *Clinical Child Psychology and Psychiatry* (14):251–71.

Kant, I. *Critique of Pure Reason.* Translated and edited by Paul Guyer and Allen W. Wood. Cambridge: Cambridge University Press, 1998.

Kernberg, O. (2014). Innovation in psychoanalytic education. *New Associations*: Issue 16: Autumn 2014, British Psychoanalytic Council.

Krantz, J. and Gilmore, T.N. (1990). The splitting of leadership and management as a social defense. *Human Relations* 43(2):183–204.

Lanyado, M. (1996). Winnicott's Children: The holding environment and therapeutic communication in brief and non-intensive work. *Journal of Child Psychotherapy* 22(3):423–43.

Law, D. and Jacob, J. (2015). *Goals and Goal Based Outcomes (GBOs): Some Useful Information*, 3rd edn. London: CAMHS Press.

Leach, P. (2004). Mothers as Managers. *Newsletter of the Association for Infant Mental Health (UK)*, 4(1):9–10.

Leichsenring, F., Rabung, S. and Leibing, E. (2004). The efficacy of short-term psychodynamic psychotherapy in specific psychiatric disorders: A meta-analysis. *Archives of General Psychiatry* 61:1208–16.

Lemma, A., Target, M. and Fonagy, P. (2011a). The development of a brief psychodynamic intervention (Dynamic Interpersonal Therapy) and its application to depression: A pilot study. *Psychiatry: Biological and Interpersonal Processes* 74(1):41–48.

Lemma, A., Target, M., Fonagy, P. (2011b). *Brief Dynamic Interpersonal Therapy*. Oxford: OUP.

Luborsky, L. (1984). *Principles of Psychoanalytic Psychotherapy: A Manual for Supportive-Expressive Treatment*. New York: Basic Books.

Luyten, P. and Blatt, S.J. (2007). Looking back towards the future: Is it time to change the DSM approach to psychiatric disorders? *Psychiatry: Biological and Interpersonal Processes* 70:85–99.

Malan, D.H. (1963). *A Study of Brief Psychotherapy*. Social Science Paperbacks. London: Tavistock Publications.

Mann, J. (1973). *Time-limited Psychotherapy*. Cambridge, MA: Harvard University Press.

Maton, K.J. (2000). Making a difference: The social ecology of social transformation. *American Journal of Community Psychology* 28(1):25–57.

Maton, K.J., Perkins, D.D. and Saegert, S. (2006). Community psychology at the crossroads: Prospects for interdisciplinary research. *American Journal of Community Psychology* 381(2):9–21.

Menzies-Lyth, I. (1988). *Containing Anxiety in Institutions: Selected Essays, Vol. 1*. London: Free Association Books.

Menzies-Lyth, I. (1989). *The Dynamics of the Social: Selected Essays, Vol. 2*. London: Free Association Books.

Midgley, N., Anderson, J., Grainger, E., Nesic-Vuckovic, T. and Urwin, C. (eds). (2009). *Child Psychotherapy and Research: New Approaches, Emerging Findings*. London: Routledge.

Midgley, N. and Kennedy, E. (2011). Psychodynamic psychotherapy for children and adolescents: A critical review of the evidence base. *Journal of Child Psychotherapy* 37(3):232–60.

Midgley, N. and Vrouva, I. (eds) (2013). *Minding The Child: Mentalisation-Based Interventions with Children, Young People and their Families*. London and New York: Routledge, Taylor and Francis.

Miller, G. (1997). Building bridges: The possibility of analytic dialogue between ethnography, conversation analysis and Foucault. In: Silverman, D. (ed.) *Qualitative Research: Theory, Method and Practice*. London: Sage Publications, pp.24–44.

Miller, S. and Sambell, K. (2003). What do parents feel they need? Implications of parents' perspectives for the facilitation of parenting programmes. *Children and Society* 17(1):32–44.

Minuchin, S. (1974). *Families and Family Therapy*. Cambridge, MA: Harvard University Press.

O'Fallon, L.R. and Dearry, A. (2002). Community-based participatory research as a tool to advance environmental health sciences. *Environmental Health Perspectives* 110(2):155–9.

Philpot, T. (2011). The parental poverty trap: Interview with Frank Field, *Young Minds Magazine*, Issue 110 February/March 2011.

Powell, B., Cooper, G., Hoffman, K. and Marvin, B. (2014). The Circle of Security Intervention: *Enhancing Attachment in Early Parent-Child Relationships*, 1st edn. New York: The Guilford Press.

Pozzi, M.E. (2003). *Psychic Hooks and Bolts: Psychoanalytic Work with Children Under Five and their Families*. London: Karnac Books.

Pozzi-Monzo, M., Lee, A. and Likierman, M. (2012). From reactive to reflective: Evidence for shifts in parents' state of mind during brief under-fives psychoanalytic psychotherapy. *Clinical Child Psychology and Psychiatry* (17)1:151–64.

Prilleltensky, I. (2005). Promoting well-being: Time for a paradigm shift in health and human services. *Scandinavian Journal of Public Health* 33(66):53–60.

Rawlins, M.D. (2008). De Testimonio: On the evidence for decisions about the use of therapeutic interventions. *The Harveian Oration of 2008, Royal College of Physicians*.

Rawlins, M.D. (2011). *Therapeutics Evidence and Decision Making*. RSM Books. London: Hodder Arnold.

Rawson. P. (2002). *Short-term Psychodynamic Psychotherapy: An Analysis of the Key Principles*. London: Karnac Books.

Read, J. and Bentall, R.P. (2012). Negative childhood experiences and mental heath: Theoretical, clinical and primary prevention implications. *British Journal of Psychiatry* 200(2):89–91.

Reeves, C. Creative Space (2003). A Winnicottian Perspective on Child Psychotherapy in Britain. Paper presented at a Workshop of the European Psychoanalytic Psychotherapy in the Public Sector Conference, Stockholm 2003, published in *Insikten No. 4 September, 2003*.

Rubio, D.M. (2010). Defining translational research: Implications for training. *Academic Medicine* (85)3:470–75.

Rutter, M. (2002). Nature, nurture and development: From evangelism through science toward policy and practice. *Child Development* 73(1):1–21.

Satir, V. (1967). *Conjoint Family Therapy*. Palo Alto, CA: Science and Behaviour Books.

Scheff, T.J. (2003). *Routines in human science: The case of emotion words*. www.soc.ucsb.edu/faculty/scheff/I.html.

Schmidt Neven, R. (1995). Developing a psychotherapy clinic for children, parents and young people at a large paediatric hospital in Australia. *Journal of Child Psychotherapy* 21(1):91–120.

Schmidt Neven, R. (1996). *Emotional Milestones: Development from Birth to Adulthood*. Melbourne: Australian Council for Educational Research.

Schmidt Neven, R. (2002). Integrative therapy: The dialogue with the unheard child. *Psychotherapy in Australia* 8(4):54–62.

Schmidt Neven, R. (2005). Under-fives counselling: Opportunities for growth, change and development for children and parents. *Journal of Child Psychotherapy* 31(2):189–208.

Schmidt Neven, R. (2008). The promotion of emotional wellbeing for children, parents and families: What gets in the way? *Educational and Child Psychology* 25(2):8–18. British Psychological Society, 2008.

Schmidt Neven, R. (2010). *Core Principles of Assessment and Therapeutic Communication with Children, Parents and Families: Towards the Promotion of Child and Family Wellbeing*. London and New York: Routledge, Taylor and Francis.

Schmidt Neven, R., Anderson, V. and Godber, T. (2002). *Rethinking ADHD: An Illness of Our Time: Integrated Approaches to Helping Children at Home and at School*. Crows Nest, NSW: Allen and Unwin.

Schore, A.N. (1994). *Affect Regulation and the Origin of Self*. Hillsdale, NJ: Lawrence Erlbaum.

Schore, A.N. (2012). *The Science of the Art of Psychotherapy*. New York: W.W. Norton.

Selvini-Palazzoli, M., Boscolo, L., Cecchin, G. and Prata, G. (1978). *Paradox and Counter Paradox: A New Model in the Family in Schizophrenic Transaction*. New York: Jason Aronson.

Shedler, J.K. (2006). That Was Then, This is Now: An introduction to contemporary psychodynamic therapy. Available from: www.psychsystems.net/Publications/Shedler: pp.1–47.

Shedler, J.K. (2010). The efficacy of psychodynamic psychotherapy. *American Psychologist* 65(2):98–109.

Shefler, G. (2000). Time-Limited Psychotherapy with Adolescents. *Journal of Psychotherapy Practice and Research* 9(2):88–99.

Sifneos, P. (1992). *Short-Term Anxiety Provoking Psychotherapy: A Treatment Manual*. Hoboken, NJ: Blackwell.

Skynner, R. (1996). *Family Matters: A Guide to Healthier and Happier Relationships*. London: Cedar.

Stanley, F., Richardson, S. and Prior, M. (2005). *Children of the Lucky Country: How Australian society has turned its back on children and why children matter*. Sydney: Pan Macmillan, Australia.

Stern, D. (1977). *The First Relationship: Infant and Mother*. The Developing Child Series: Cambridge, MA: Harvard University Press.

Sugarman, R. (2004). Review of R. Schmidt Neven, V. Anderson and T. Godber, Rethinking ADHD (2002): *Metapsychology Online Book Reviews*.

Target M. (2012). Testing Times: The demand for evidence and the future of child analytic work. Annual British Psychoanalytical Society Research

Lecture, November 2012. In: Troupp, C. and Catty J. (2012). *Bulletin of the Association of Child Psychotherapists*, Issue 238:17–21.

Timimi, S. (2002). *Pathological Child Psychiatry and the Medicalisation of Childhood*. Hove: Brunner-Routledge.

Troupp, C. and Catty, J. (2012). Discussion of lecture by Mary Target, November 2012 on 'Testing Times: The demand for evidence and the future of child analytic work.' (Annual British Psychoanalytical Society Research Lecture). *Bulletin of the Association of Child Psychotherapists,* Issue 238:17–21.

Trowell, J. and Miles, G. (2011). *Childhood Depression: A place for psychotherapy*. London: Karnac.

Trowell, J., Rhode, M. and Hall, J. (2010). What does a manual contribute to work with depressed people? In: Tsiantis, J. and Trowell, J. (eds). *Assessing Change in Psychoanalytic Psychotherapy of Children and Adolescents*. London: Karnac.

Trowell, J., Rhode, M. and Joffe, I. (2009). Childhood depression: An outcome research project. In: Midgley, N., Anderson, J., Grainger, E., Nesic-Vuckovic, T. and Urwin, C. (eds). *Child Psychotherapy and Research: New Approaches, Emerging Findings*. London: Routledge.

Trowell, J., Joffe, I., Campbell, J., Clemente, C., Almgvist, F., Soininen, M., Koskenranta-Aslto, U., Weintraub, S., Kolaitis, G. and Tomarar, V. (2007). Childhood depression: A place for psychotherapy. An outcome study comparing individual psychodynamic psychotherapy and family therapy. *European Child and Adolescent Psychiatry* 16(3):157–67.

Trowell, J., Rhode, M., Miles, G. and Sherwood, I. (2003). Childhood depression: Work in progress. *Journal of Child Psychotherapy* 29(2):147–70.

Tsiantis, J. and Trowell, J. (eds) (2010). *Assessing Change in Psychoanalytic Psychotherapy of Children and Adolescents*. London: Karnac.

Von Hayek, F.A. (1974). The Pretence of Knowledge. Nobel Prize Lecture, 11 December 1974. Available at: nobelprize.org/nobelprizes/economics/laureates/1974/hayek-lecture. Html (accessed 31 March 2016).

Walker, G. (2015). Interview with Gail Walker. *The Bulletin of the Association of Child Psychotherapists,* Issue No. 261, June 2015: 7–8.

Watzlawick, P., Beavin Bavelas, J. and Jackson, D.D. (1967). *Pragmatics of Human Communication: A Study of Interactional Patterns, Pathologies and Paradoxes*. New York, London: W.W. Norton.

WHO (1992). *The ICD-10 Classification of Mental and Behavioural Disorders*. Geneva: World Health Organization.

Winnicott, D.W. (1958). *Collected Papers: Through Paediatrics to Psychoanalysis*. London: Tavistock.

Winnicott, D.W. (1964). *The Child, the Family and the Outside World*. Harmondsworth: Penguin.

Winnicott, D.W. (1965). *The Maturational Processes and the Facilitating Environment*. London: Hogarth.

Woolf, S.H. (2008). The meaning of translational research and why it matters. *Journal of the American Medical Association* 299(2):211–13.

Index